BOSTON CELTICS

Where Have You Gone?

MIKE CAREY AND
MICHAEL D. McCLELLAN

www.SportsPublishingLLC.com

ISBN: 1-58261-953-0

Publishers: Peter L. Bannon and Joseph J. Bannon Sr.
Senior managing editor: Susan M. Moyer
Acquisitions editor: Mike Pearson
Developmental editor: Doug Hoepker
Art director: K. Jeffrey Higgerson
Dust jacket design: Joseph T. Brumleve
Interior layout: Joseph T. Brumleve and Kathryn R. Holleman
Imaging: Kenneth J. O'Brien, Dustin Hubbart, Heidi Norsen, and
    Kathryn R. Holleman
Photo editor: Erin Linden-Levy
Media and promotions managers: Letha Caudill (regional),
    Randy Fouts (national), Maurey Williamson (print)

Printed in the United States of America

Sports Publishing L.L.C.
804 North Neil Street
Champaign, IL 61820

Phone: 1-877-424-2665
Fax: 217-363-2073
www.SportsPublishingLLC.com

To former Celtics team physician Dr. Arnold Scheller and his family. As a Special Forces medical officer, Dr. Scheller's service to his country in the Gulf War, Iraq, Afghanistan, and Croatia make him a true American hero.

— M.C.

To Graham and Melanie—I love you both dearly. And to my parents, for always believing.

— M.M.

CONTENTS

ACKNOWLEDGMENTS

The authors would like to thank Celtics Vice President of Media Relations Jeff Twiss, UCLA media relations VP Bill Bennett, Derek and Renate Vogel, Rick and Donna Carlisle, Preston and Joan Carlisle, Fabio Anderle, Bill Sharman, all the ex-Celtics players who were so cooperative in taking the time to recount their days in Boston, Greg and Joan McGinty, Bill Walton, Tommy and Helen Heinsohn, Daniel and Michelle Ainge, attorneys Valerie Pawson and George Hailer, Don and Jen Worden, Dr. Ron Kolodziej, Gail Weisberg, Dr. Jim Katz, and our very patient editor Doug Hoepker, as well as Courtney Hainline, our marketing manager.

Where Have You Gone?

KEVIN GAMBLE

Hang Time

The sports world has no shortage of Hollywood-style success stories, of players who have overcome great odds to fulfill a dream, overcome tragedy or capture the imaginations of millions. These stories are the lifeblood of competition, and the reason fans keep coming back for more. And for each of these sporting miracles, there are hundreds of other stories—of failure, disappointment, and despair—that serve as cautionary tales for the next generation of athletes. Lost in between are the stories of those who simply hang in there and never give up. They persevere, refusing to be cast aside, insisting that their talent is good enough to share the stage with the greatest athletes in the world—even when logic and common sense dictate otherwise.

Kevin Gamble knows what it's like to persevere. The one-time high school standout took a circuitous route to the Boston Celtics and the NBA, playing basketball at both the junior college level and Division I levels before taking his dream to the CBA and, eventually, to the Philippines and back again. He never doubted himself, convinced that he was capable of not only reaching the NBA, but also of forging a long, successful career at the game's highest level. Today the multifaceted Gamble is the head coach at the University of Illinois at Springfield, the owner of a thriving Athlete's Foot franchise, and the driving force behind

AP/WWP

KEVIN GAMBLE

College: Iowa '87 | Height: 6'5" | Weight: 210 lbs. | Position: Guard
Years with Celtics: 1988-'89 through 1993-'94

Notes: Selected by Portland in the third round of the 1987 NBA Draft.
Played two seasons in the CBA before getting a call from the Boston Celtics.
Excellent play at end of 1988-'89 season (subbing for an injured Dennis Johnson)
led to long-term contract with Celtics.

a successful real estate venture aimed at revitalizing the inner city in his hometown.

"I just finished up my third year of coaching," Gamble says from his office at the Athlete's Foot. "I'm trying to get some experience as a coach, and this is a unique opportunity because we're building the program from the ground up. The goal is to get the University of Illinois at Springfield basketball program to the NCAA Division I level."

From the ground up is exactly how Gamble built his career, one proverbial brick at a time. A star at Springfield's Lanphier High, Gamble led the Lions to a state championship in 1983. Even then, success was the result of years of preparation.

"We knew we were going to have a pretty good ball club when we were seniors in high school," he says. "We had the same players that we had in the eighth and ninth grade, so it was a good nucleus of players. A state championship was something that was always in our minds, and we were fortunate enough to go out and get the job done."

Few questioned Gamble's ability at the high school level, but many college recruiters wondered whether he had Division I potential. Undeterred, Gamble enrolled at Lincoln Junior College following graduation, where he played for two seasons under the guidance and tutelage of head coach Alan Pickering.

"Growing up, my parents were very important to me, and I looked up to them in many ways. The thing I remember about Coach Pick was of him being the first role model of my adult life. He helped to mold me, and helped to show me what I needed to do to make it at the college level. He taught me how to be a better basketball player, which I appreciate greatly, but more than that he helped me to become a man."

Pickering's basketball influence on Gamble could be summed up in one word: defense. The wise coach knew that his star pupil could produce on offense, but he also knew that Gamble's ticket to Division I basketball rested with his commitment to playing tenacious defense. Gamble soaked in the many lessons learned during those two seasons at Lincoln, and a year later found himself playing basketball for the University of Iowa. Head coach George Raveling, however, wasn't overly impressed by what he saw; Gamble's first year in Iowa City was spent mostly on the bench, watching the action and wondering if his time would ever come, because player and coach failed to see eye to eye on nearly everything related to basketball.

As if by divine intervention, Tom Davis replaced Raveling at season's end. Gamble responded to the change in a big way. Suddenly the focal point of the offense, he led the Hawkeyes to a 30-5 record and the NCAA tournament regional finals.

"It was a great experience being part of a great university like Iowa. My first year was fun off the court, but on the court it was very disappointing. Not that Coach Raveling and I didn't get along; it was just that he didn't see me as the player that Coach Pick saw me as, or the player that my high school coach saw me as. At Lanphier I played shooting guard and small forward, and at Lincoln I was primarily a shooting guard. But once I got to Iowa, Coach Raveling saw fit to play me at power forward with guys like Ed Horton and Brad Lohaus—much bigger guys than I was, both in height and weight. I wish I could have redshirted, because I averaged a total of six minutes per game that year.

"Thankfully, Coach Davis came in that next year and started everyone off with a clean slate. He told us that nobody had positions, and that everyone on the team had to earn their playing time. I practiced hard and won two positions—the two guard and small forward spot—but ended up mostly playing the two. Coach Davis is probably the main reason that I made it to the NBA. Because of him I had a pretty good senior season, and a pretty good [NCAA] tournament, and ended up being drafted by the Portland Trail Blazers in the third round."

Gamble's stay in Portland was brief—nine games in total—before he was waived and forced to persevere yet again. But while he left Oregon without a job, he also left convinced that he could compete in the NBA. Battling players such as Clyde Drexler and Terry Porter in training camp helped. Grasping the offensive and defensive schemes as rapidly as he did also helped. But understanding that he'd been caught up in a numbers game may have been the biggest boost of all.

"They had some guys on the injured list," Gamble says matter-of-factly. "John Paxson and Ronnie Murphy were the key guys out with injuries. Paxson was an established veteran, and Murphy was the team's first-round draft choice. So I knew that the team would make some changes when these guys were healthy enough to play."

Gamble went to the Detroit Pistons' camp the following summer, only to find himself in a situation eerily similar to that in Portland. The CBA—Continental Basketball Association—was the next obvious angle to work, and Gamble did so without hesitation.

"I just kept plugging away," he remembers. "I played a full CBA season, where I played pretty well—I think I averaged 20 points and 10 rebounds—and everyone there stressed that I had to play defense to make it to the NBA. So that's what I worked on."

The Milwaukee Bucks invited him to their camp prior to the start of the 1988-'89 season. Released just two weeks later, he played in the Philippines for a month, returned to the CBA for a 12-game stint with Quad Cities, and then received a welcome call from the Boston Celtics. This time Gamble was ready.

"I played 12 games for Quad Cities," he says, "and I was averaging close to 30 points a game. That's when I got the call from the Boston Celtics."

An injury to Larry Bird gave Gamble his chance. He was determined to stick. Still, he knew that it would not be easy; the Celtics roster was populated with Hall-of-Fame talent, legendary players like Bird, Kevin McHale, and Robert Parish, as well as quality talent like Dennis Johnson, Danny Ainge, and Brian Shaw. Gamble logged 17 "DNP—Coaches Decision" that first year, the shorthand for "benchwarmer." It looked like the team would make him available in the expansion draft to either Orlando or Minnesota, but then he turned in seven strong minutes in a road win over Philadelphia. He followed that by playing exceptionally well in place of an injured Dennis Johnson during the final six games of the regular season.

"It was exciting for me," Gamble says. "Ironically, it was another injury that provided my opportunity to play. 'DJ' rolled his ankle in

Atlanta—everyone knew that it was really bad. We didn't know if he was going to miss the last six games, but we knew the next game was out of the question.

"The next game was against Cleveland. Coach [Jimmy] Rodgers comes into the locker room, goes over the pregame talk, and tells us who the Cavaliers are starting. He tells us that they're starting Larry Nance, Brad Daugherty, Ron Harper...he tells Brian Shaw that he's guarding Mark Price, and then he tells me that I'm guarding Harper. That was the first time that I heard that I was going to be starting a ball game. Of course, everybody knows Ron. He's known for his offensive and defensive play. It was exciting but nerve-wracking. Somehow I had a terrific game. I had something like 20 points, 10 assists, and seven rebounds."

By the following season Gamble was firmly established as an integral part of the Boston Celtics. It was a time of transition for the team, as the Big Three of Bird, Parish, and McHale were starting to decline, and young players such as Shaw and Reggie Lewis were being groomed for future greatness. Gamble would go on to play five full seasons for the Celtics, before retiring with Miami in '96.

"I'll always be a Boston Celtic. There were so many great times. I remember signing my first big contract with the team. Red just couldn't understand how a guy who couldn't rebound could command a million-dollar contract," Gamble, who was given the nickname "Oscar" by teammate Danny Ainge, says with a chuckle. "I remember that before games, Red would come into the locker room and talk about the days when he coached. The guys would be trying to get their ankles taped, and Red would be sitting on the trainer's table, telling his stories...the time would be ticking, and you're trying to get ready to play. But those were special times. For Red to take the time to talk to you, it showed you how much he cared about us as players."

Today, Gamble continues to persevere, earning his stripes as a basketball coach the same way he earned them as a player. He also owns several commercial buildings in Springfield, leasing them out while working to revitalize the inner city.

"I stay busy, that's for sure. Right now my primary focus is on coaching. I want to build the Springfield program from the ground up, make sure that it is both successful and respected, and also try to take what I learn to the next level."

If his remarkable playing career is any indication, Kevin Gamble will hang in there and do just that.

Where Have You Gone?

ARTIS GILMORE

A Gentle Giant

He is perhaps the greatest living player eligible for induction into the Naismith Memorial Basketball Hall of Fame. His résumé is sensational: 24,941 points, 16,330 rebounds, and 2,497 blocks spread over 17 professional seasons and two leagues. Still, Artis Gilmore finds himself on the outside looking in, awaiting a telephone call that is embarrassingly overdue. The list of accomplishments is nearly as long as the shadow cast by this 7'2" giant with the low-key personality and intimidating post presence. Criminal, this wait; displayed annually on each voter's ballot is a high school All-American with a trip to the NCAA championship game under his belt, an ABA superstar who posted 12 solid NBA seasons after that league folded, an 11-time All-Star with a streak of 640 consecutive games played. And yet here he is, forced to lobby for his own enshrinement, as if he were a fringe talent undeserving of the game's highest honor. Absolutely, positively criminal.

But if any of this bothers Gilmore, he is not the type to wear his frustration on his sleeve. He knows as well as anyone that life goes on, and that sooner or later he will receive his just due. Until then, he is happy to continue doing what he does best, which is to play the role of family man to perfection. With his youngest son, Artis Gilmore II, still in school, much of his energy is spent readying his son for life in the real world.

AP/WWP

ARTIS GILMORE

**College: Jacksonville '71 | Height: 7'2" | Weight: 265 lbs.
Position: Center | Years with Celtics: 1987-'88**

Notes: Signed by the Boston Celtics to a free agent contract on January 8, 1988. Provided backup support at the center position to Robert Parish for the rest of the season and on into the '88 NBA playoffs.

"My wife, Enola, and I have worked really hard to give our kids a quality education and to keep them focused on their studies," he says by telephone from Louisville. Gilmore is in town for the Kentucky Derby, where he and his Kentucky Colonel teammates will be honored for their 1975 ABA championship. As hard as it is for him to believe, 30 years have passed since that exciting win over Indiana. "Time flies, especially when you are involved with your children. Artis II is a good student, and we want to make sure that he continues to make good grades like he is making right now. That's our primary focus."

Now living in Jacksonville, Florida, Gilmore is more than a stay-at-home dad. He works for W.W. Gay Mechanical Contractor, Inc., in the area of private development. The company is based in Jacksonville, where he once led Jacksonville University to the NCAA title game against mighty UCLA.

"We do commercial estimating, HVAC, design/build, a whole host of things," he says. "I am currently focused on customer relations and private development, and I have played a part in turning W.W. Gay into the largest mechanical contractor in the southeast. It is very satisfying work."

Gilmore's long and illustrious basketball career may be behind him now, the rebounds and blocks replaced by Rolodexes and boardrooms, but it remains a frequent topic of conversation. Small wonder: when you are world famous for your exploits on the hardwood—and over seven feet tall to boot—the subject tends to come up from time to time.

"Every day," he says matter-of-factly when asked if people still recognize him. Whether opening doors of potential clients or simply thrilling those who remember his stellar play, Gilmore is approached wherever his goes. "People recognize me everyday, and they want to talk about some aspect of my career."

And while the player affectionately known as the "A-Train" may have seen his last NBA stop as a member of the Boston Celtics, this during an abbreviated 47 game stint during the 1988-'89 season, Gilmore holds to Red Auerbach's credo of "Once a Celtic, always a Celtic."

"While my role was limited with the Celtics, I certainly enjoyed my time spent with the Celtic organization. For the first time in my NBA career, I was able to play deeper into the playoffs than I had my previous 11 years. And it was truly a professional organization. Today, many of the other NBA organizations are similar in the way they treat the athlete, but that wasn't always the case. The level of professionalism wasn't the same, and the other franchises have had to play catch-up. Something as simple as uniforms is a prime example; the Celtics always made sure that the uniforms were clean and ready for the players, whereas this task was the player's responsibility everywhere else that I played. That has all changed now. All NBA franchises take care of the uniforms."

Much has changed for Gilmore since growing up poor in rural Chipley, Florida. Back then his family could barely make ends meet, and there were times when food was hard to come by. Jobs were scarce, race relations tense, and the future seemed as bleak as the craggy roads connecting this small town of 5,000. Still, his parents were convinced that young Artis could make something of himself. They instilled in him a strong value system, with a premium on things such as morals and character, and a belief that education was the key to a better life than the one they had lived. Gilmore paid attention. He attended an all-black school—this was pre-integration—and he stayed out of trouble, sidestepping the dual temptations of drugs and alcohol while pursuing his first love, football. A growth spurt, coupled with a minor football injury, turned Gilmore's athletic focus to the hardwood. The family moved to nearby Dothan, Alabama, prior to his senior year of high school, and the 6'9 1/2" boy responded by being named a third-team All-American. The sky seemed the limit, yet it took a two-year stop at Gardner-Webb Junior College in Boiling Springs, North Carolina, for Gilmore to reach his full athletic potential.

"I ended up at Gardner-Webb simply because my grades were very poor," he says. "It was a two-year school at the time, but by the end of my second year it had become a four-year program. The coaches wanted the players to stay, but several of us decided to move on. I looked at Jacksonville [University], and decided that it was right for me."

Playing in Jacksonville meant playing closer to home, and this was a huge plus for the gifted pivot man. Now 7'2" with the musculature of a young Wilt Chamberlain, Gilmore instantly transformed the Dolphins into a collegiate power, as the team went 27-2 during his senior season and reached the NCAA championship game. Awaiting them: legendary coach John Wooden and the mighty UCLA Bruins. Gilmore staked Jacksonville to an early lead, but Wooden was able to adjust his lineup and neutralize the Dolphins' advantage underneath the basket. It proved to be the difference in the game.

"We played well," Gilmore says, reflecting on what could have been. "We were not intimidated, and we certainly didn't idolize UCLA. We were ready to compete, but I'm not so sure that we played our best basketball. Sidney Wicks had an extraordinary game against me. There was always a question of some of the shots that were blocked, and whether they were goaltending, but Sidney was very aggressive in going to the basket. He deserves credit for playing so well."

Despite the loss, Gilmore did nothing to diminish his standing as the top center in collegiate basketball. He averaged 20 points and 20 rebounds during those two seasons in Jacksonville, and found himself coveted by both the NBA and the ABA. The Chicago Bulls drafted him, as did the Kentucky Colonels of the ABA, and Gilmore was faced with his first big decision as a professional.

"I had a very young attorney, and what I thought was a very good support group in Jacksonville. They advised me that [signing with the ABA] was a great opportunity to do some things right away for my mother and father, who were certainly very special people in my life. So I wanted to make sure that I could give something back to my parents. At the time, the ABA was the quickest way to do that."

Gilmore's transition to professional basketball was seamless. He led the Colonels to a 68-14 record that first year, earning the Rookie of the Year and the Most Valuable Player awards for his outstanding play. Statistically, he finished 10th in the league in scoring, first in rebounds, and first in field-goal percentage, but it was the intangibles that really made the difference. Gilmore was an intimidating presence underneath the basket, forcing opposing teams to alter their game plans—and opposing players to alter their shots.

"I was still in college when I started to believe I could succeed at the professional level," Gilmore says. "There was a gentleman named Bones McKinney. He worked with me, and told me that I could very easily make the transition from college to the pros."

McKinney, a former Boston Celtic, proved to be prophetic in his analysis of the young center. Gilmore played five seasons in the ABA, producing staggering statistical numbers and leading the Colonels to the ABA Finals twice, both against Indiana. By 1975, Gilmore and the Colonels were champions of the ABA.

"We had a very good coach in Hubie Brown," recalls Gilmore. "We had Dan Issel, Louie Dampier, Ted McClain, and Bird Averitt to name a few. It was a very competitive, very smart group of players, and we were able to play very well together."

The ABA would fold a year later. Ironically, the Bulls would have the first overall pick in the dispersal draft. In a draft that included such talent as Moses Malone and Maurice Lucas, Chicago wasted little time in snatching up one of the best big men in basketball: Gilmore. A slow start that first season—the Bulls would open with 13 consecutive defeats—was more than offset by the strong finish, as Gilmore led Chicago to 20 wins in the final 24 games. During this stretch he erupted for 32 points, 17 rebounds, five assists, and four blocks against the Seattle Supersonics, and 29 points and 23 rebounds against the Philadelphia 76ers.

If there were any doubters concerning Gilmore's ability, he proved them wrong by posting numbers comparable to those put up while playing in the ABA. He averaged no less than 17.8 points during his six seasons with the Bulls, playing in all 82 games five times. His durability as a professional was remarkable; Gilmore played in a mind-boggling 670 consecutive games, a number almost unheard of when it comes to the warriors who battle underneath the boards.

"Robert Parish was another iron man," Gilmore says, referring to his former Celtic teammate. "He was an extraordinary player, and I remember the transaction that sent him from Golden State to the Celtics. …He seemed to be a perfect fit. It turned his whole career around. It turned him into an extraordinary person as well as a great, great center. He had such a good understanding of the game. He understood his role, especially playing with players like Larry Bird, Kevin McHale, Nate Archibald, and Danny Ainge. To be compared to him in any way is very flattering."

While Gilmore was named an All-Star in four of his six seasons as a Bull, the team struggled to advance in the playoffs. He asked to be traded following the 1981-'82 season. The San Antonio Spurs were the recipient of this good fortune, as Gilmore gave that franchise five solid years in the paint. The first season, Gilmore and the Spurs reached the Western Conference Finals, where Kareem Abdul-Jabbar and Magic Johnson awaited.

"The Lakers were very talented, well-coached, and deep," he says. "We played them hard—I think I played Kareem as well as anyone in the league—but we just couldn't stop them."

After five seasons in San Antonio, the team was in a rebuilding mode. Gilmore was traded back to the Bulls, where he played 39 games during the 1987-'88 regular season. He then found himself traded again, this time to Boston.

Does Gilmore have a fond memory of his time spent as a Celtic?

"To this day, Larry Bird remains one of my closest friends. We talk by phone quite frequently. As a member of the Boston Celtics, we had a chance to reflect on some of our earlier times together, like the time we spent together in Panama City. Larry was at Indiana State then. Even further back, when he was living in French Lick, Larry would come to the Kentucky Colonels games, so we had a chance to talk about that. So spending time with Larry was very special for me."

MEL COUNTS

The Good Life

At just a shade over seven feet tall, Mel Counts covered considerable real estate as he patrolled the Boston Garden paint during the mid-sixties. A one-time backup to Bill Russell, Counts today still thinks in terms of real estate, only now in a very literal sense; the player nicknamed "Goose" is a successful broker for an independently owned Prudential Real Estate franchise.

"I've been a realtor for 28 years," says Counts. "Listing and selling properties, investing in properties, things of that nature. It's something that I really enjoy doing. I've been blessed in that regard, no question about it."

Counts has been blessed in many ways. A father of five and grandfather of 13 ("With one on the way," he says proudly), Counts left basketball following the 1975-'76 NBA season and returned to his native Oregon, where he is very active in his church and also in various civic organizations. A vigorous pro-life supporter, an avid hiker, and fisherman, Counts has maintained a positive, fulfilling lifestyle that has left an indelible mark on those who know him. He frequently speaks to church groups and kids groups, and often takes along the gold medal that he won in the 1964 Olympics. He hopes that it inspires those to excel in the

MEL COUNTS

College: Oregon State '64 | Height: 7'0" | Weight: 230 lbs.
Position: Center | Years with Celtics: 1964-'65 through 1965-'66

Notes: Member of the 1964 gold medal-winning men's Olympic basketball team.
Won two NBA Championships as a member of the Boston Celtics.
Teammate of both Bill Russell and Wilt Chamberlain.

endeavors of their choosing, and that it serves as a reminder that, with the right combination of skill and faith, anything is possible.

Indeed. Born on October 16, 1941, in Coos Bay, Oregon, Counts found his inspiration in the small town environment and the natural wonders found only in that part of the country.

"I remember when it rained, you didn't have to worry about your top-side getting wet. It was your bottom-side you had to worry about, because the rain came at you sideways—so an umbrella didn't do you a whole lot of good," Counts says, with a laugh.

At the time, Coos Bay was the top exporter of lumber in the world. It was also a fishing community, and Counts developed a passion for angling at a very early age. He still hunts and fishes with a lifetime friend from his childhood, and says that his current love—hiking—can be traced directly to his youth. It was a different era, a simpler era, one in which Counts and his friends could safely hitch the three miles from his home to downtown Coos Bay, where he would catch the latest feature in the local movie house before hitching back home in the dark.

With so much to do outdoors, basketball didn't become a real interest until Counts was in the fourth grade. He took to the sport quickly. A natural athlete with good coordination and an innate feel for the game, he worked hard to develop a solid foundation based on the fundamentals.

"One of the best coaches I ever had was my fourth, fifth, and sixth grade coach," he says. "He was a true mentor, and his enthusiasm for the game really helped me to stay interested. He was constantly drilling us with basketball fundamentals. What he did for me then really set the stage for the rest of my life."

Counts went on to become the most accomplished basketball player in the history of Marshfield High School, earning a scholarship to play collegiate hoops for the legendary Slats Gill. Gill, who had taken the 1949 Oregon State team to the Final Four, would do so again in 1963 with Counts as the centerpiece of the Beaver attack. Counts, then a junior, would earn All-America honors for his efforts, a feat that he would repeat in his senior season.

"To me, Slats was one of the greatest college coaches ever," says Counts. "To have the opportunity to play in the Final Four was something special. I think that nine of the 13 players were from the state of Oregon. Terry Baker was on that team—he had won the Heisman Trophy and was also *Sports Illustrated*'s Sportsman of the Year. Steve Pauley was a decathlon champion. We had two or three baseball players. We didn't have the best record of any Oregon State team, but we had a real cohesive group, and we came together at the right time. We made it to the Final Four, lost to Cincinnati, and then lost to Duke in the consolation game. Back then you played two games regardless. It was just a special time and a wonderful experience to have. To represent the state of Oregon was quite a privilege and quite an honor."

The 1964 Olympic Games were held in Tokyo, and Counts was selected to play for legendary college coach Hank Iba. As hard as it may be to fathom, the U.S. men's basketball team was considered something of an underdog going into the 18th Olympiad. The Soviet Union had made great strides with its basketball program. The world, it seemed, was catching up to America.

"The writers wrote us off," he says, still perturbed by the sleight after all of these years. "They said that we weren't going to get the job done. We didn't have a Jerry West, or an Oscar Robertson, or a Walt Bellamy. These guys went on to become superstars in the NBA. We didn't have anybody on our team like that. But we did have Hank Iba and a great group of assistant coaches.

"We went to Pearl Harbor and worked out for three weeks. We worked out twice a day, for three hours a pop, and when it came game time we were ready. We were extremely well prepared and extremely well conditioned. We went in with confidence, tradition, and the idea that the sports writers had written us off. Our goal was to represent our country to the best of our ability, and that's exactly what we did. We won the gold medal and proved everybody wrong."

The Boston Celtics selected Counts in the first round of the 1964 NBA draft with the ninth pick. He arrived in the best shape of his life. He had heard the horror stories of Red Auerbach's training camps, and of how the Celtics were annually the best-conditioned players in the league. Following those grueling practices at Pearl Harbor, he felt more than ready to hold his own.

"That first training camp felt like boot camp," Counts says, smiling. "The first three days we didn't shoot the basketball. In fact, back then they didn't know as much about nutrition as they know now, and about how the body recovers from exercise. We'd go full bore from ten until 12, and then from two until four, with hardly a drink of water. There wouldn't be any breaks. Now they practice in the morning and in the evening, which makes more sense. It gives the body more time to recover.

"But the fact that they ran so much in training camp certainly gave the Celtics an edge. Having Bill Russell, the greatest defensive player in the history of the game, didn't hurt, either," recalls Counts with a chuckle. "It all played into Red's up-tempo offense, which was predicated on the fast break. Those training camps were quite an experience."

The Celtics won a seventh consecutive championship during Counts's rookie campaign. The season was noteworthy for two other reasons as well: team founder Walter Brown's passing on September 7, and John Havlicek's famous steal during the 1965 Eastern Conference Finals.

"The guide wire supporting the backboard almost cost us that game against the Sixers," Counts recalls. "I remember a conversation between Red Auerbach and Bill Russell prior to that series, and the decision was made to leave the guide wire in place. Well, it was a really close game and Russell had to inbound the basketball. Sure enough, he hit that wire and gave the ball back to Philadelphia under their basket. I thought, 'Oh no, this is it,' and then Havlicek came out of nowhere to steal the basketball. He was a smart, smart player. He grabbed the ball, made the pass, and the rest is history."

The Celtics won their seventh consecutive championship a series later. For Counts, it was his first championship at any level.

"At the time you don't really take it all in," he says, "but as time goes on it becomes more meaningful. Now I can look at my Celtic ring or my Celtic watch, and say, 'Hey, I was on a world championship team.' I've been very blessed and very fortunate to play on those teams."

The Celtics would win it all again a year later. Counts was then traded to Baltimore for versatile forward Bailey Howell, who would go on to win a pair of titles of his own. The stay in Baltimore was short-lived, however, as Counts soon found himself headed to the Lakers. Suddenly, he was playing on the other side of the NBA's most intense rivalry.

"It was great. I had the opportunity to be in a championship situation with the Celtics, and I wanted to accomplish the same thing with the Lakers. It was also special because I had the pleasure of playing with the two greatest centers in the history of the NBA—Bill Russell and Wilt Chamberlain. So it was a very satisfying experience."

These days, Counts still shares his basketball experiences with others. The Celtics remain a very big part of who he is, even though he spent just two of his 12 seasons with the team. He won his only championships there, and he teamed with some of the greatest players ever, during arguably the greatest dynasty in the history of professional sports. His has been the good life, and he knows it.

"I've been blessed," he says. "How many people can say that they've played with guys like Russell, Havlicek, Sam Jones, Tommy Heinsohn, K.C. Jones, and Satch Sanders? I'm extremely lucky in that regard, and I've got the rings to prove it."

JEFF JUDKINS

Fill in the Blank

Jeff Judkins certainly seemed destined to have a long and productive career as a Celtic. As a rookie, the 1978 second-round draft choice who had helped lead the University of Utah to two NCAA berths, was so impressive during camp that he earned a spot in Boston's regular rotation rather than learning the Celtics' system by observing from a seat at the end of the bench. Playing almost 19 minutes a game, he shot better than 50 percent as a swingman, averaging 8.8 points, 2.4 rebounds, and a steal per game. By far, he was Boston's most consistent and enthusiastic reserve.

"I was thrilled to be part of the Celtics' tradition," Judkins says. "It was just so exciting for a young guy like me to be playing with such great players as Dave Cowens, Nate Archibald, and Cedric Maxwell. And, like everyone else, I was very much aware that Larry Bird would be joining the team the next season."

Under new head coach Bill Fitch, Judkins's minutes decreased in 1979-'80 because Boston had added versatile guard Gerald Henderson and defensive stopper M.L. Carr to its roster. However, his overall play remained at a high level. For the second straight year, he shot better than 50 percent from the field and 82 percent from the foul line.

"We ended up with a 61-21 record and made it to the conference finals in 1980 [before being eliminated by Philadelphia]," he says. "It was

APWWP

JEFF JUDKINS

College: Utah '78 | Height: 6'6" | Weight: 185 lbs.
Position: Guard | Years with Celtics: 1978-'79 through 1979-'80

Notes: Second-round draft choice (the 30th pick overall) by the Boston Celtics in 1978, the same year the Celtics selected Larry Bird with the sixth overall pick overall. Selected by the Dallas Mavericks in the NBA expansion draft on July 28, 1980.

such a fun season that I was one hundred percent sure I wanted to spend my entire career with Boston. I was going to be a free agent, so I wanted to let management know I had no plans to sign anywhere but with the Celtics.

"Late in the season, I walked into Red Auerbach's office and sat down with him and Coach Fitch. I told them, 'This is the only place I want to be. If you sign me to another contract, I don't care about the money. You can write any dollar figure you want on my contract, and I'll sign it. We can do it right now. That's how much I want to be a part of this team.' Auerbach and Fitch looked at me as if I was absolutely out of my mind. I mean players just don't tell teams they don't care about what they're making."

Auerbach told Judkins he'd talk to him about his contract situation once the season ended. Unfortunately for the 23-year-old, there was an expansion draft to be held that May to stock the NBA's newest team, the Dallas Mavericks. Boston left 32-year-old Pistol Pete Maravich and Judkins unprotected in the expansion draft. The Mavs selected Boston's second-year outside shooter.

"I knew Dallas was going to take me," he says. "Pistol Pete was ready to retire and almost everyone Dallas was planning on taking was 26 years old or younger."

In his brief stay with the Celtics, Judkins—who was all-state in basketball, football, and baseball as a Utah high school player—became good friends with Bird.

"As everyone knows, Larry was so tough, so strong, and so fearless whenever he was on the court. But I saw another side to him when he visited me in Utah. My family had a houseboat on Lake Powell and we'd go cliff diving. My friends and I would dive off 20-to-30-foot cliffs. Larry refused, telling us, 'I ain't gonna kill myself.' So, we found a little cliff, maybe eight or nine feet above the water. He still refused, despite the fact that we just unmercifully kidded him about being more scared than a five-year-old.

"The next day, we ran into a little storm while we were cruising around on the houseboat. Water came into the boat, but not a heck of a lot. Well, Larry literally runs to get a life preserver. He's turning white as a ghost, almost in panic mode. We're all giving him grief because he's the guy who supposedly never shows fear. Then he tries to recover by saying, 'Hey, I got a ten-year career ahead of me, and I'm not going to sit here and wait to drown while this leaky piece of junk goes under.' He'll probably deny he chickened out of the cliff diving and wasn't afraid when we ran into the storm—but it's all true."

Although selected by Dallas, Judkins never played a game for the expansion club. As a free agent as of July 1, 1980, he opted to sign with the Jazz, for whom he would play 62 games during his lone season in Utah. He would go on to play as a seldom-used reserve in Detroit and Portland before retiring after the 1982-'83 season.

"I considered myself a good team player," he says. "I always felt Boston was the perfect fit for me. I'm not knocking the teams I played for after I left the Celtics, but my game just wasn't the same, because I just never felt comfortable with the style of basketball that was played by the teams I was with."

After his NBA career was over, Judkins entered the business world and eventually became an executive with Safelite Auto Glass, the nation's leading auto glass repair and replacement service company. He has also run basketball camps during the summers. In 1989 he accepted an offer from University of Utah head coach Rick Majerus to join his coaching staff, where his primary duties were recruiting and advance scouting. Among some of his prize recruits were Keith Van Horn, Andre Miller, Michael Doleac, Hanno Mottola, Trent Whiting, and Britton Johnsen.

Although Majerus had a reputation of being a demanding boss, Judkins enjoyed his ten years as an assistant coach at Utah. "I learned a lot. Coach [Majerus] is a great teacher of every aspect of the game," he says. "But in 2000 when BYU offered me the chance to become director of basketball operations, along with being an assistant coach in men's basketball, I thought it was the right time to move on."

Shortly before his second year at BYU, the ex-Celtic accepted the BYU women's head coaching position. Since taking over the program, Judkins's teams have earned two invites to the NCAAs, and advanced once to the Sweet Sixteen. In addition the BYU women also secured a berth in one NIT tournament. Overall, his teams have compiled a four-year record of 77-46, having never suffered a losing season.

"Women's basketball reminds me of how NBA teams played in the '80s, because women are slower than men and can't easily take their defender off the dribble, they rely on teamwork to find ways to get easy baskets. That's how the game of basketball should be played," he says. "I can't stand to watch much NBA basketball or even some men's college games because it's all one-on-one stuff. There's no passing, no cutting off picks, no setting screens. It's just not my kind of basketball. It's boring, plain and simple."

However, Judkins leaves open the possibility of coaching at the NBA level or running a men's college program. "It would depend on the quality of the organization, the type of people who run the team, and the style of play," he says. "If all of those factors were positive in my eyes, I'd give the opportunity serious consideration."

Jeff and his wife, Mary Kaye, reside in the Provo, Utah area and are the parents of five children—Jessica, Jordan, Jenna, Jaime, and Jaxson. Among his hobbies are water skiing, horseback riding, hunting, golf, softball, and watching "my daily couple of hours of ESPN."

JOHN BACH

Still A Coach

When John Bach signed a $5,000 contract to play for the Celtics back in 1948, he thought he would give basketball a try for a couple of years and then enter the business world. "But," says the former naval officer who served at Okinawa, "basketball never managed to find a way get rid of me."

At age 81, Bach is still hanging around basketball, now as an assistant coach with the Chicago Bulls, where he's in charge of the team's defensive strategy. He has been a coach in the pro ranks for the last 26 years, having previously spent 28 years as a college head coach. His memories of his stay in Boston have not faded with time.

"You hear people talk about the Celtics family. Well, it was true even when I played for them," the Fordham grad says. "[Boston owner] Walter Brown treated everyone so tremendously. Like when he found out I was getting married, he gave me a $500 bonus. Totally unexpected, but it was typical of how Mr. Brown operated. Then there was [public relations director] Howie McHugh. He felt it was part of his job to watch over the players. If you had a problem, no matter how small or large, Howie was right there to help you solve it. The entire front office staff always made you feel special."

JOHN BACH

**College: Fordham '48 | Height: 6'2" | Weight: 180 lbs.
Position: Forward | Years with Celtics: 1948-'49**

Notes: Drafted in the first round by Boston in 1948. Averaged 3.5 points per game
in his only season in the NBA. Head coach of the Golden State Warriors from 1983-'86.
Chicago Bulls assistant coach during Michael Jordan's first
three championship seasons (1991-'93).

In those days, the team practiced at Boston University, and many of
the players, including Bach, lived in a large room just down the corridor
from the gym. "It was a spartan existence. We paid two dollars a night to
rent a cot," he recalls. "You'd get up in the morning, have some cereal,
walk about 20 steps and start scrimmaging."

At the time, the Celtics were coached by Alvin "Doggie" Julian, who
would go on to coach at Dartmouth for 17 seasons and be elected to the
Basketball Hall of Fame.

"He was the type of guy who could scare the hell out of you," says
Bach, who along with guard Tommy Kelly were the only rookies on the
1948-'49 team. "He'd really push you to your limits. He'd always let you
know that if you didn't produce, he could find someone who could.

"He used to tell us, 'You have to always play hard. You have to love
the game. If you don't, you'll find yourself out driving a cab somewhere.'
Well, a few years later, I was walking down a street in New York and this
taxi driver pulls over and starts beeping his horn at me. I look over and it's
my old Boston teammate, John Ezersky. First thing he says to me is 'Tell
that SOB Julian that his prediction came true.'"

The six-foot-three Bach played only one season for the Celtics,
coming off the bench to score 3.5 points a game. He was cut in training
camp the following season when rookie Joe Mullaney, who would
eventually enjoy a highly successful pro and college coaching career, beat
him out for the final roster spot.

"Then I decided to play for Hartford in the Eastern Basketball League. We got $100 a game, and we usually played three or four games a week," Bach remembers. "The competition was excellent. One team, the New York Rens, an all-black team, had about five players who could have been excellent NBA players had it not been for the league's racial discrimination. In fact, the Rens had a six-foot-three shooter and passer named Pop Gates, who was as good an all-around player as anybody in the NBA. Today he's in the Hall of Fame.

"The Rens faced racial bias in every city they played, yet they maintained the highest degree of professionalism. Today, I have a picture of the team hanging in my office, and I tell all the black players that they owe a debt to those guys because they paved the way for blacks to play in the NBA. One of the Ren players, Chuck Cooper, was among the first blacks drafted by the league, chosen by Walter Brown and the great Red Auerbach."

Shortly after the 1949-'50 Eastern League season ended, Bach was offered the opportunity to be the head coach at Fordham. "I really didn't think I was qualified for the job, because I had no experience," he says, "but the athletic director convinced me to give it a try." In Bach's first five years on the Fordham bench, the Rams compiled an overall record of 95-39, never losing more than nine games in any season.

"Everything about the situation was great," he says. "I had some great teams there. But in 1967 I decided to leave because I wasn't making enough money to support my wife and five children. I accepted an offer to coach Penn State, where I received a better salary. I also was given tenure for teaching, which paid extra."

The strangest day in Bach's coaching career came in 1972. "I was an assistant to Henry Iba on our Olympic basketball team," he says. "That was, of course, the team which supposedly lost to the Soviet Union in the final seconds because of several controversial rulings by the officials. I've never seen such a complete injustice."

After guiding the Nittany Lions to a 122-121 record over a ten-year span, Bach asked for a leave of absence. "I knew I probably would never go back to college coaching, because all the recruiting had burnt me out," he explains. "I knew I would never want to deal with recruiting again. I had my pilot's license, so I went to work flying planes for the Piper Corporation."

When then-Golden State Warriors general manager Pete Newell asked Bach to become head coach Al Attles's top assistant in 1979, Bach jumped at the offer.

"Pete and Al were both people I knew and respected," he says. "I had only been away from the game for a year, but I really missed coaching. Now I'd be back—and on the pro level, something I hadn't done yet. It was the challenge I was looking for."

Shortly before the start of the 1983-'84 season, Attles moved into the front office, and Bach was promoted to head coach. "We had three tough years because we weren't very deep," he says of the experience. "Larry Smith was a monster at power forward. Purvis Short, with that rainbow shot of his, and Sleepy Floyd gave us outside scoring. Beyond that, though, we lacked consistency."

When he was dismissed by the Warriors in the summer of '86, Bach faced a major decision. "I could play the waiting game and sit at home until someone offered me a head coach's job or I could find an assistant's position. I knew that if I waited for a head coaching opening, it would probably be with a team that was having big-time problems. That's how it always works out in the pros. In military terms, it boiled down to this: Did I want to be the leader of a barbarian outfit or a captain in the Roman Army?"

Bach chose the latter, joining Phil Jackson (and, of course, Michael Jordan) in Chicago. When the Bulls reeled off three straight championships in 1991, '92, and '93, it was Bach who designed and directed the defense.

"Those were great, great times," he says. "You know, I had always thought Oscar Robertson was the one NBA player who stood above everyone who ever played the game. Michael, however, was better than Oscar. He was absolutely peerless."

Leaving Chicago in 1994, Bach spent two seasons in Charlotte, two in Detroit, and three in Washington as an assistant. "Two years ago, I was planning on retiring," he says. "But then one of my former players, [Bulls general manager] Johnny Paxson, called me and asked me to join [new head coach] Scott Skiles's staff. I couldn't say 'no' to Johnny."

The upcoming 2005-'06 season may be Bach's last. "I'm 81 years old. I think 81 is a nice round number," he says. Bach, who lives in Chicago suburb with his wife, Mary, admits that he's had about as full of a career as anyone could hope for. With health concerns in his past, he senses that maybe now is a good time to slow down.

His favorite souvenir all his years in coaching is not one of the championship rings he earned in the NBA, but rather a letter he once received from Bob Cousy when the Hall of Famer was head coach at Boston College.

"I was coaching Fordham and we had just beaten BC at their place. It was a big win for us because they had a darn good squad," Bach says. "A few days afterward, a letter arrived at my office. It said, 'Last time I saw you, you were being lifted to the heavens. Congratulations on a job well done. Best wishes, Bob.' I was amazed that someone as busy as Cousy could take the time to write such a nice message. I still have that letter, which is my most treasured basketball possession."

CONNER HENRY

Dream Job

Imagine doing something so well that you are granted membership into one of the world's most exclusive fraternities, where only one in every 10,000 is selected to perform before an audience of millions. Now imagine yourself sharing the stage with the preeminent talent in your chosen profession, at a time when history unfolds before you in unprecedented abundance. You are *there*, in the middle of it all, plying your trade in the company of greatness.

Who wouldn't want to be you? Your stage is one of sport's holiest cathedrals. Your teammates are the reigning world champions, and you have joined them in their quest to repeat and build a dynasty. Your debut comes off as scripted in Hollywood, with shots falling from almost impossible distances and the throaty, hometown crowd roaring its approval. Future hall-of-fame players slap you on the back, wish you well, and accept you as one of their own. And when that magical game is finally over, you walk away secure in the fact that you've made the most of a golden opportunity.

Your name is Conner Henry, and you have *arrived*.

For legions of basketball junkies, simply making it onto the Boston Celtics roster is the dreamiest of dream jobs. It is a franchise steeped in history, a standard-bearer in the realm of championships, an icon so

AP/WWP

CONNER HENRY

College: California-Santa Barbara '86 | Height: 6'7" | Weight: 195 lbs.
Position: Guard | Years with Celtics: 1986-'87 through 1987-'88

Notes: Drafted by the Houston Rockets in the fourth round of the 1986 NBA draft.
Signed to the first of two consecutive ten-day contracts by the Boston Celtics on
January 1, 1987. Made his Boston Garden debut six days later, going four-of-five from
behind the arc. Re-signed for the remainder of the season on January 22, 1987.
Waived on November 30, 1987.

resplendent in its deal-closing that even now, nearly 20 years removed from its last title, the rest of the NBA can only look up at those 16 banners with a mixture of aspiration and envy. Now imagine being a Boston Celtic when the roster is populated with names such as Bird, McHale, Parish, and Walton. These men are the Mount Rushmore of low-post play, and here you are, feeding the ball to them in practice. In games they find you for spot-open threes, confident that you will bury the shot if given the opportunity. This would be enough for almost anyone, but there are more surprises to come; perhaps no defending champion in NBA history battled as much adversity as the 1986-'87 Boston Celtics, as a valiant playoff run would leave them two games short of their coveted repeat.

You and I can only dream of the perfect alchemy of place and circumstance. Henry lived it. He was there the night that Larry Bird stole the ball from Isiah Thomas, and he was there to witness that dagger of a baby hook by a man named Magic. Henry can tell you all about June basketball in the fabled Garden, about the heat and the rats and the obstructed-view seating that gave the place its charm.

Conner Henry's journey from unabashed hoop addict to solid NBA player began in Claremont, California, where his father worked as a college professor at Claremont McKenna College. Today, Granville Henry is recognized by the school as an emeritus professor.

"My father began teaching there as a math professor in 1959," Henry says admiringly, as he reminisces from his office on the Claremont McKenna campus. Now an assistant basketball coach for the Stags, Henry has come full circle. "I literally grew up at Claremont McKenna. Our house was directly behind the football field, which meant that you had to walk through the campus to get to it. I was involved in athletics very early in my life, serving as a ball boy in all three major sports at the age of five, so athletic competition came very naturally to me."

It was here that Henry gained unfettered access to the athletic facilities, gravitating to the basketball court in large part because of his lithe frame. He played for long hours, sometimes with others, sometimes alone, always dreaming of one day making it onto the game's biggest stage. His idol was "Pistol" Pete Maravich, and Henry molded his game after the flashy guard, landing at UC Santa Barbara with a repertoire of fancy passes and a reputation for deadly long-range accuracy. He was a starter from Day One, overcame an injured knee during his junior season, and finished atop the career assists mark in the school's record books.

"The injury was very frustrating," Henry points out. "It occurred during practice. I was in a full sprint when someone clipped my heel from behind and I fell hard on my left knee. I was lucky in one respect, because I only stretched the ligament and didn't actually tear it. The doctor equipped me with a steel knee brace so that I could continue to play basketball. The brace was considered top of the line back then, but by today's standards it was quite archaic. But it enabled me to continue playing, which in my eyes was the most important thing at the time. I didn't redshirt that season but, in retrospect, I probably should have taken the time to recover. I just didn't fully understand the dynamics of the injury. As it was, the team's starting point guard was also dragging that big, cumbersome brace up and down the court."

Brace or no brace, Henry excelled on the basketball court. As a senior, he displayed both poise and deadeye marksmanship in consistently leading UC Santa Barbara in a number of statistical categories. And although the Gauchos would never be confused with national power UCLA, Henry & Co. made things interesting for a number of ranked foes.

"We played the University of Houston when the team was ranked Number 1 in the country and also boasted Phi Slamma Jamma," remembers Henry. "They came to Santa Barbara with Hakeem (then known as Akeem) Olajuwon and Clyde Drexler, and everyone expected them to run us out of our own building. Our tallest player was six foot seven, and he had to battle Olajuwon on the blocks. It was a great atmosphere. The Thunderdome was sold out, and they were still letting people in. The fire department must have turned its eye in another direction for this game.

"Houston jumped out to a huge lead, and was up by 19 points at halftime. We played incredibly well after intermission and nearly pulled off the upset, losing by two points."

The Houston Rockets drafted Henry in the fourth round of the 1986 NBA Draft—the same draft in which the Celtics would draft Maryland star Len Bias. Henry played just 18 games in Texas before landing in Boston, where he quickly made a name for himself as a three-point specialist. Close friends with Dennis Johnson, Henry found himself on the Celtics' roster courtesy of the NBA's 10-day contract. Facing the Milwaukee Bucks in his inaugural home game with Team Green, Henry drained his first shot—a three-pointer—and energized the Boston Garden faithful with his hard-nosed play. He would finish the contest by converting four of five from behind the arc, finally exiting the court as the sellout crowd showered him with the spontaneous chant of "Ten more days."

"It was a magical night," recalls Henry. "I had no idea something like that might happen, although we were playing the Milwaukee Bucks and I had a feeling that I'd get into the game. I was very excited, very nervous, but once I got into the game I was able to settle down. I got my legs underneath me, which also helped, but the main thing was being a member of the Boston Celtics. When you have players like Larry Bird, Robert Parish, and Kevin McHale to throw the ball to, you don't feel as much pressure to go in and make things happen. They command so much attention that good movement and ball rotation will put you in a position to succeed. And that's what happened. I got open, and the first one went in. That relaxed me, and I was able to flow with the game the rest of the way. I kept moving and kept getting looks, and the shots kept going in.

"I'll never forget the chants from the fans. It was incredible. …Everyone on the team made it a point to congratulate me, which certainly made me feel like part of the Boston Celtics."

Timing, as they say, is everything, and Henry's presence on the team coincided with some of the most memorable moments in Celtics history. Take Bird's steal from Isiah Thomas, for example. Regarded as one of the greatest players in NBA history, Henry had a front-row seat for Larry Legend's game-saving—and, quite possibly, series-saving—theft. Only John Havlicek's legendary steal ranks higher in terms of late-game heroics by a Boston Celtic.

"From the sideline all we could do was hope for a foul or a steal," says Henry, "but with so little time left, the likelihood of either happening was slim to none. A foul, maybe, but a steal? At the time you don't realize the true magnitude of something like that—you're overcome with excitement, but you just don't fully grasp the historical significance of that play. It's only later that you realize what you've been a part of. When I see the play today, I can look at it and know that I was involved. It's a great feeling."

That Celtics-Pistons series was also known for its intensity. Bill Laimbeer's takedown of Bird set the tone, as did Robert Parish's retaliation one game later. Who can forget the sight of Laimbeer, knocked to the floor, bloodied, while the Boston Garden faithful roared in approval?

"The NBA became a different place because of that series," he says. "Detroit's bruising style of play had never really existed at that level. The referees were letting them define their style, which was very physical and based on intimidation. The smothering defenses that you see today have their roots in what the Pistons were doing back then. Every possession was critical, and defending the basket became even more important than actually scoring on the offensive end."

Bird's steal kept Henry's dream season alive, catapulting him directly into the 1987 NBA Finals. The Lakers were the last hurdle left, but they were a deep, talented, and rested team. The Celtics, by contrast, were worn out. Every series had been a battle. Players were hurt. The bench was thin. Still, much was hanging in the balance when Magic Johnson hit the infamous baby hook. That shot turned the series irrevocably in the Lakers' favor, and Henry's own magical run would soon be over.

"Magic got the ball, turned, did that drive whirl and let go with the baby hook," says Henry. "Kevin and Robert played it perfectly, both of them extending as far as they could to defend the shot, but the ball went over both of them and into the basket. It was a terrible blow to us, and we felt it long after the game was over. Instead of squaring the series at two games apiece, we had to win that third game in the Boston Garden and then win two more in Los Angeles. Given the physical condition of our team, it was just too much to expect."

For Henry, life has come full circle; now the associate director of career counseling at Claremont McKenna, the former Boston Celtic is back home and doing what he loves. It is his new dream job, but the memories of the old one are still very much alive. He can close his eyes and see Robert Parish, hobbled by a severe ankle sprain, battling Bill Laimbeer and the Detroit Pistons on one leg. He can see Kevin McHale gutting out another superb performance on a broken foot. He can see Bird's steal and Magic's hook, and he can take satisfaction in knowing that he was there as hoop history was being written.

The rest of us should be so lucky.

GLENN McDONALD

Two Minutes of Fame

If not for his clutch shooting performance in the third overtime of what is almost universally regarded as the most exciting game in NBA history, Glenn McDonald might just be another obscure bench player whose name and stats appear among the hundreds listed on the Celtics' all-time roster. Instead, the reserve guard became a Boston legend in a matter of less than two minutes.

The heroics took place on June 4, 1976, in Game 5 of the Celtics-Suns playoff finals, which was knotted at two games apiece. In a game that had numerous bizarre moments, Boston seemingly appeared to have won the game in the second overtime when John Havlicek nailed a jumper as time was expiring to give the Celtics a 111-110 advantage. However, as the fans celebrated by mobbing the court, referee Richie Powers ruled that there were still two seconds remaining because Suns guard Paul Westphal—the former Boston Celtic—had signaled for a timeout immediately after Havlicek's basket. Phoenix, though, had no timeouts left and was assessed a technical foul, which Celtic guard JoJo White converted.

Although now down by two points, Phoenix was able to put the ball into play from halfcourt, thanks to Westphal's quick thinking. On the ensuing play, Suns forward Garfield Heard took the inbounds pass from

GLENN McDONALD

**College: Long Beach State '74 | Height: 6'6" | Weight: 198 lbs.
Years with Celtics: 1974-'75 through 1975-'76 | Position: Forward**

Notes: First-round draft choice (the 17th pick overall) of the Boston Celtics in 1974. Member of one NBA championship team (1976). Waived on October 21, 1976.

teammate Curtis Perry and fired in an 18-foot jumper to tie the score at 112-112 and force still another overtime.

Boston seemingly had lost its momentum. And when starting power forward Paul Silas became the fourth Celtics player to foul out with less than two minutes left in the third overtime, head coach Tommy Heinsohn had few options. He gambled by bringing in the 6'6" McDonald instead of the more experienced and taller Steve Kuberski.

"I wanted fresh legs out there," explains Heinsohn. "Both teams were exhausted. Glenn was the fastest guy I had. All I told him was, 'Mac, run 'em every chance you get.' Kuberski was a better rebounder than Glenn, but, in that situation, I wanted someone who could outrun the opposition."

Having hit only five of 23 shots up to that point in the playoffs, McDonald was surprised to get the opportunity to play at such a crucial stage of the game.

"As soon as Silas fouled out, I told Kuberski, 'You're going in. Take off your warm-ups,'" remembers McDonald. "But when Heinsohn motioned for me instead, I was ready. As a bench player, you prepare for a moment like that. You practice hard every day, hoping you'll be on the court in that type of situation. Plus, I wasn't totally cold. I had played seven or eight minutes in regulation, just coming in a few times to give guys a breather."

With 1:35 remaining in the third overtime, McDonald put in a layup to give the Celtics a 120-118 lead. On the next Celtics possession, a John Havlicek pass set up the guard for a smooth, 10-foot fallaway jumper over

Phoenix guard Dick Van Arsdale, increasing Boston's lead to four. Fittingly, it was McDonald who snared a defensive rebound, drew a foul, and confidently sank two free throws to clinch a nerve-wracking 128-126 victory for the Celts.

"The free throws were easy. I just stepped to the line with the attitude that I couldn't miss. Both of them went in pretty easy. After the game, it didn't really hit me that people would focus on my contributions as much as they did," McDonald says. "I knew I had played well, but we still were only up 3-2 in the series. It wasn't until later that night when I couldn't get any sleep that I realized how much of an impact my points had in that game. Suddenly it was like I was in awe of what had taken place."

After the Celtics earned their 13th championship by defeating the Suns, 4-2, McDonald fully realized precisely how much he had accomplished during Game 5 when he earned his two minutes of fame. "I'd hear the replay of Johnny Most's calls on the radio, or I'd pick up a newspaper and see my picture on the front page of the sports section," he recalls. "Fans would come up to me and just start cheering. It was just an unbelievable time for me."

An All-American at Long Beach State, McDonald was selected by the Celtics in the first round of the 1974 draft. "Until my senior year, I was strictly a defensive type of player," he says. "Some scouts were comparing me to Don Chaney, because I was tall for a guard, had long arms, and loved to pressure whomever I was guarding. When Lute Olson took over as head coach at Long Beach before my last year there, he told me to always shoot when I got open. He really gave me the confidence to be more aggressive on offense. I scored fairly well and started to get noticed by some scouts."

As the draft approached, McDonald thought the Bucks would take him with the 18th pick. "I knew they had seen me play a couple of times when I had played well," he says. "I had no idea that the Celtics [who were selecting one slot ahead of Milwaukee] had an interest. Obviously, I was absolutely elated that Boston knew about me and wanted me."

During his rookie season, McDonald played less than seven minutes a game, shooting 39 percent. He still has a clear memory of his initiation into the league.

"One of my first games was against the Bucks in Milwaukee," he says. "Being young and being a rookie, I thought I had a nice running jump hook. Well, I made the mistake of trying to use that shot as I went into the lane. The ball barely left my hand when Kareem [Abdul-Jabbar] took one step towards me and slapped it over our bench and way up into the crowd. Every guy on the bench was howling with laughter. Even Heinsohn was doubled up. When something that embarrassing happens and you're on the court, there's nowhere to hide."

During the 1975-'76 regular season, the quiet reserve began to earn more minutes. "I used him quite a bit because he was one of those high-energy guys that every coach likes to have come off the bench," recalls Heinsohn. "I liked bringing him in when we had a lead because he could force turnovers, block shots, and rebound well. I could use him to guard either a small forward or a big guard, whoever was a bigger scoring threat."

So when McDonald finished the year by helping the Celtics win a title, he had every reason to be optimistic about his future. Ironically, though, the series against Phoenix would mark McDonald's final games with the club.

"I had gotten married in the offseason and was really looking forward to playing another season, maybe more, in Boston," he says. "But the team was making a lot of changes. Don Nelson was retiring, Silas was leaving to play for Denver, Sidney Wicks and Curtis Rowe were coming in. For whatever reasons, they made the decision to cut me in training camp."

The Bucks quickly signed McDonald as a temporary replacement for guard Fred Carter, who was out for a month with an injury. After playing just nine games, he was released. The next year McDonald was invited to the Suns training camp.

"[The Suns] had just drafted Walter Davis, so I knew the odds were against me," he says. "At that point, I decided I didn't want to go year to year not knowing where I'd be playing or even if I'd be playing. I didn't think it would be fair to my wife to always be uncertain of whether an NBA career would work out for us."

Opting to play overseas, McDonald signed a one-year guaranteed contract with Alvik in Stockholm, Sweden. That team won the Swedish championship and played in the European Cup competition. The adventure gave McDonald the opportunity to travel all over the European continent. It also gave him the motivation to snatch up a new job offer the following year. McDonald decided to spend one more season in pro ball—in the Philippines.

"I discovered it was a very competitive league," McDonald recalls of his time in the Asian league. "My wife and I enjoyed living there, so we just kept going back—for eight more seasons."

In 1987, he retired and returned to his alma mater of Long Beach State where he became a part-time men's basketball assistant for two years. He moved on to become a full-time assistant coach for the women's team for two years and women's head coach for four seasons. Since 1996, he has been director of Intramurals at the college.

In addition to his 18-year career at Long Beach State, McDonald was L.A. Sparks head coach Michael Cooper's top assistant when the team won back-to-back WNBA titles in 2001 and 2002.

"It was another great time for me. To get a chance to be a part of a great pro team and a great staff was so rewarding," he says. "I'm just grateful my school was kind enough to have allowed me to take time off during the summers to accept the Sparks job."

Glenn and his wife, Renee, have been married 29 years and reside in the Long Beach area. The couple has two children: Michael, a former Stanford basketball player, and Alexi, a former University of Washington volleyball player.

"Every so often at one of [Long Beach State's] basketball games the scoreboard video screen will show a video clip of me during that Celtics-Suns fifth game," he says. "Afterwards, a couple students will usually come up to me and say, 'Gee, Mr. McDonald, I didn't know you played for Boston.' It really lets me know how old I'm getting."

DINO RADJA

International Flavour

When the Celtics drafted Jugoplastika Split forward Dino Radja with the 40th pick of the 1989 draft, the Croatian star had substantial self-doubt about whether he could be successful in the U.S.

"At that time, you could count the number of Europeans in the NBA on one hand," Radja says. "At the time I was drafted, there were three guys who were doing well. There was Drazen Petrovic, Vlade Divac, and Arvydas Sabonis. But I knew those guys. They were all great, great players. I didn't know if I was in their class. To play in the NBA and fail, that was my biggest fear."

But the Celtics did not share Radja's concerns. "We first saw Dino during the '88 Olympic preliminaries, and he was outstanding," says former Boston general manager Jan Volk. "Then we saw him again in the McDonald's Classic. He played against us and was matched up quite a bit against Kevin [McHale]. Not only was he not intimidated, he shot the ball very confidently and did a reasonably good job guarding Kevin, which, of course, was about as tough an assignment as anyone could have."

As the 1989 draft approached, the Celtics decided to take a calculated gamble and use their second-round selection to choose the draft-eligible Radja, who had led Split to the European Cup championship. "The problem was that Split told us that he had another year remaining on his

AP/WWP

DINO RADJA

College: None | Height: 6'11" | Weight: 255 lbs.
Position: Forward | Years with Celtics: 1993-'94 through 1996-'97

Notes: Second-round draft choice of the Boston Celtics in 1989
(played in Italy from 1990-'93). Signed on July 9, 1993. Member of the
NBA All-Rookie Team in 1993-'94. Waived on July 16, 1997.

contract and under no circumstances would they agree to a buyout," says Volk. "We tried every legal recourse possible, but we couldn't gain his release."

So Radja returned to Croatia and completed his contract. However, he was still not convinced that his playing style and scoring ability would necessarily bring him success at the NBA level.

"I was comfortable in Europe. I knew I was among the top two or three players there, and I knew I could make an excellent salary in Europe," says Radja, who speaks fluent English, Italian, and Greek. "If I went to the U.S., it would mean a lot of adjustments. The NBA game itself was more physical, because the players were bigger and stronger than in Europe. I also would have had to get used to an entirely different culture. In the end, I decided to play another season in Europe and then, maybe, think of the NBA."

Although Radja signed a contract with the Celtics in August of 1989, Split and Boston, as part of the deal, agreed that the six-foot-11 forward would play one more year for Jugoplastika before joining then-head coach Chris Ford's club. After he completed a successful 1989-'90 season with Jugoplastika in which his team reached the European Cup final four, Radja was still reluctant to play in the NBA.

"I was playing well," Radja remembers. "I was making a great salary. The thing about playing in the NBA was that there were so many unknowns."

The Celtics decided not to force Radja to come to Boston. Instead, they allowed him to play for Il Messaggero Roma for three years in return for cash. In his first season there, he averaged 18.1 points and 10.1 rebounds while shooting an incredible 59 percent from the field. For his achievements, he was voted second best player in Europe, behind only Toni Kukoc. In his second season in the Italian League he averaged 20.2 points on 54 percent shooting. The highlight of his year came at the Olympics when Croatia won the silver medal.

"If it wasn't for the U.S. Dream Team, we would have won the gold. I believe that," he says. "The talent we had was unbelievable. Our frontline was me and Kukoc at forward, and [then-Celtic Stojko]

Vrankovic at center. Our shooting guard was [Drazen] Petrovic. But that U.S. team—with Larry Bird, Michael Jordan, Magic Johnson, Charles Barkley, David Robinson, Patrick Ewing, Karl Malone, and John Stockton—they destroyed us twice. Those were our only two losses."

Following the Olympics, he returned to Virtus Roma (formerly Il Massaggero) for one final season in which he averaged 21.5 points. "I knew I was ready to play for the Celtics because more and more Europeans were not only playing in the NBA but doing well," he says. "I wasn't satisfied with how my team played against the United States in the Olympics, but the one thing I found out from the experience is that I could play on that level and do okay."

In his four years with Boston, Radja did better than merely "okay." In his first season, he averaged 15.1 points and 7.2 rebounds on 52 percent shooting, earning a spot on the NBA's All-Rookie second team. The following year he led the team in both rebounding and blocked shots while finishing second in scoring. His best overall production came in 1995-'96 when he led the team in both scoring (19.7) and rebounding (9.8).

"Things were all coming together for me," he says. "I was able to do the things I wanted to offensively. I had learned how to get just the right position to box out and rebound. I felt good about my game. The team was rebuilding, and everyone kept telling me I'd be a big part of the process."

However, injuries forced Radja to miss 57 games in his fourth—and final—season with Boston. Following that season, Rick Pitino took over as head coach and president of the Celtics.

"I went to Pitino and asked him if I fit into his plans," said Radja. "With a new coach, I obviously wanted to know what he thought of my game. I loved playing for Boston and just wanted to find out if there was any possibility I might be traded, because I had heard some rumors. Pitino looked me right in the eyes and said, 'Dino, don't worry. You're going to be a big part of our offense. When we run a set play, the ball is going to go through you.' I left the meeting feeling great. Five days later, I found out I was being traded to Philadelphia [for Clarence Weatherspoon and

Michael Cage]. I can't tell you how much I felt betrayed. Either Pitino lied to me or something changed in a matter of a few days."

The Philly trade, however, fell through when Radja did not pass the 76ers physical. "I didn't want to leave Boston. After the way I had been deceived, the only place I would have gone was Orlando or maybe Miami," he says. "I had made up my mind that I would rather go back to Croatia than play somewhere I didn't want to be."

Still, Radja had three years remaining on his guaranteed contract. Whether he could pass another team's physical was debatable. If he couldn't, Boston would have to pay the forward his entire remaining salary. Eventually, Radja and the Celtics agreed on a buyout. He headed back to Europe, where he played four seasons in Croatia and three in Greece.

"Once I discovered the Celtics had sent me to Philly, I knew that if I failed the 76ers physical, Pitino didn't want me back in a Celtics uniform." Radja says, "But I knew I could still be a productive player. And I proved that in Europe. I put up good numbers, especially in the European Cup against the best teams.

"I'm not bitter, though. By going back and playing seven years in Europe, I probably extended my career by two or three years because teams only play 30 to 35 games a year over there. There's much less wear and tear on a player's body. You may play every five days, which gives you time to rest and let any injury heal. I was 36 when I retired. I think that's a pretty good career."

Today, Radja is the president of Jugoplastika Split, his hometown team. "In Europe, teams are run by a committee, which sort of answers to the sponsors. If you don't win, you'll probably lose some sponsors. Teams in Europe depend on sponsors for most of their income. Arenas are not large, so attendance isn't that great. There also isn't much revenue from TV or radio," he explains. "My title is president, but in Europe that really means I do what a general manager does in the NBA."

Radja, whose favorite hobby is fishing, resides in Split with his wife, Victoria. He says he has only one regret concerning his Celtics years. "I wish I had gotten the chance to play with Larry Bird as my teammate," he says. "I can't lie. There are times I think about what would have happened if I played for Boston right after I was drafted. Bird, McHale, Parish, the big three—it would have been fun for me just to watch them play together."

Radja admits that he is still contemplating a comeback, even at age 38. "Real Madrid is one team which has talked to me about playing a year or two," he says. "We talked back in July. I'm in pretty good shape, so I've been thinking it over. I'm tempted."

MARK ACRES

Class Act

Casimir Middle School is not unlike many other middle schools across the United States. Backpack-wearing students arrive via bus, many of them wearing the latest clothes, listening to their favorite music, and idolizing the best athletes in the world. They dream of being the next Michael Jordan or Mia Hamm, scoring goals and winning championships while attaining fame and fortune in the process. They thrill at the thought of meeting players from their favorite teams, and of collecting autographs along the way. Typical adolescents. The difference between the students at Casimir Middle School and most other schools is that a giant of a man walks the corridors with them, teaches their classes, and helps them stay focused and out of trouble. He is 6'11" and not far from his playing weight of 225 pounds, dimensions that came in handy during another career, this as a member of one of the greatest franchises in NBA history.

Meet Mark Acres, man-in-the-middle turned middle school teacher.

"It's very rewarding," Acres says of his work at Casimir Middle School. The one-time Boston Celtic may be decidedly "old school" to students who weren't even born when he played the game, but then Acres doesn't expect them to appreciate what it was like playing with Larry Bird, Kevin McHale, and Robert Parish.

AP/WWP

MARK ACRES

College: Oral Roberts '85 | Height: 6'11" | Weight: 225 lbs.
Position: Center | Years with Celtics: 1987-'88 through 1988-'89

Notes: Played eight seasons in the NBA.
Signed by Boston as a free agent on May 7, 1987.

"It's a different generation," he says. "These kids have their own heroes. They have their favorite players, whether it's a LeBron James or a Kobe Bryant, and they don't really care about players that they haven't seen before."

And while the Big Three may have given way to the Three Rs—reading, writing, and arithmetic—Mark Acres is still very much in tune with the NBA and what makes it so popular around the globe.

"I played in Europe for two years," he says, "and even back then you could see the influence that the NBA was having overseas. And then you look at how far the league has come today—you have players like Yao Ming from China, and Manu Ginobili from Argentina. Now even more people can identify with the players in the NBA."

Located in Torrance, California, Casimir is a melting pot of cultures and ethnicities, with Asians and Hispanics making up 67 percent of the student body. Acres clearly enjoys what he is doing, and he brings incredible diversity with him from his days as a professional basketball player. While his students may only have a passing knowledge of his accomplishments on the hardwood, they certainly appreciate what he does in his current capacity.

"I enjoy teaching," Acres says proudly. "It's something that I've always wanted to do, so I went back to school after retiring from the NBA and completed my masters in education."

The inspiration for Acres's dual loves—teaching and athletics—came from his father, Dick, who was a high school basketball coach and, later, the head coach at Oral Roberts University. Dick Acres stressed the fundamentals of the game, insisting that his son master everything from the outlet pass to the midrange jumper. Mark responded by channeling his prodigious basketball talent. He focused on one sport, becoming a true student of the game, and also one of its biggest fans. Growing up in Inglewood only served to fuel the fire.

"I was a Lakers fan growing up," he says of a childhood spent in the shadows of West, Baylor, and Chamberlain. "They were always very competitive, and their best battles were always with the Celtics—which made it interesting when I landed in Boston."

Attending Palos Verdes High School, Acres excelled at both athletics and academics. It was very much a Utopian environment, with little in the way of trouble, which left Acres free to hone his basketball skills. He was mobile for a big man, with good footwork and a nice touch around the basket, exactly the types of things that recruiters were looking for in a Division 1 basketball player. A spot on the McDonald's All-America Team didn't hurt matters, either.

"It was an honor to be selected," Acres offers modestly. "Being chosen as an All-American puts you in about the top 25 players in the country. I'm sure a few are left off that deserve to be there, but those things are beyond your control. So it was a very nice honor, and I still cherish it today. I still have my McDonald's ring, as well as some booklets from the game."

With scholarship offers pouring in, there was little doubt where Acres would end up.

"I followed my father to Oral Roberts. It was a pretty natural transition for me, because he'd been my coach for my whole life. So that part was pretty easy. I was used to his system and to the way he coached. And I knew what he expected from me."

Acres made the college leap look easy, being named to the All-America team following his freshman season. It would become an annual rite of spring; unheard of today, Acres finished his collegiate career by receiving the honor four years running.

"Earning a place on the team was very special to me," says Acres. "To be recognized once is great, but to do it at every stage, from my freshman season to my senior season—that is something I'm very proud of. And if I had to pick one that meant more than the others, I'd have to say my junior season. That was the year that we went to the NCAA tournament. It was—and still is—only the second time that has happened in school history."

Acres was drafted in the second round of the 1985 NBA draft by the Dallas Mavericks. With three first-rounders competing for roster spots ahead of him, it didn't take Acres long to realize that he was being squeezed in a time-honored NBA numbers game. He opted to play two seasons in Europe instead, where he could further prepare his game for the premiere league on the planet. It turned out to be a wise decision; rather than waiting to be cut by the Mavs and toiling in the CBA, he was able to join a team that could give him regular playing time. Instead of languishing on a bench, he was able to fill a significant role on a European playoff contender. He posted averages of 19.5 points and 10 rebounds his first season overseas, and topped that with 20 and 16 the following year. A polished Acres returned to the States in 1987.

"My first year in Europe was not a very pleasant one," Acres concedes. "I was very homesick, and I missed my family, and it just seemed like I was missing a whole lot. But then I got used to it, and knew what to expect, and it became a lot easier the second time around. I really enjoyed it. If I had the time, I'd like to get back to Europe every year."

While living in Europe may have been difficult from an emotional standpoint, there was a huge upside to plying his trade in a foreign land: free agency. Back then this didn't mean an instant avalanche of money, as it does in so many cases today, but at least it meant that Acres could contact other clubs regarding his services. And when the Mavericks selected Roy Tarpley in 1986, they effectively renounced their rights to the big man from Oral Roberts.

Acres returned in 1987 a different player—faster, stronger, and more confident in his abilities. The Celtics were still reeling from the death of Len Bias and were trying to prepare for life after Larry, Kevin, and Robert. It was a very well-timed union.

"I liked my chances of making the team," Acres says of his first training camp with the Celtics. "That was one of the reasons I left Dallas to play overseas. I wanted to join a team with an opportunity to play. With the Celtics, that opportunity existed. It was the first time I'd stuck it out and went to all the camps, including veteran camp. It was exciting, but it was also a mental and physical drain. Very demanding. You keep playing, you try to do your best, and you try not to leave anything to chance."

Larry Bird averaged a career-high 29.9 points per game during the 1987-'88 season. For Acres, guarding Larry Legend in practice was unlike anything he'd ever experienced in basketball.

"It was always a challenge," he says, laughing. "He was a fantastic scorer and an even better basketball player. You just tried to get a hand on the ball or deny him the pass. Anything to keep the ball out of his hands."

Injuries to Kevin McHale and Bill Walton opened the door for Acres and fellow rookie Brad Lohaus, and early on the duo made the most of the opportunity. But then, with the playoffs approaching, head coach K.C. Jones shortened his rotation, and both players saw their minutes shrink. But how could they complain? The Celtics were still a power in the East. Sit as they might, they were still members of the most fabled franchise in basketball, and their teammate was one of the best players to ever set foot on a court. Never was that more apparent than in Game 7 of the 1988 Eastern Conference semifinals. Most people remember it as the famous shootout between Larry Bird and Dominique Wilkins.

"What an incredible series," recalls Acres. "We had just beaten the Hawks in Atlanta in Game 6. Larry was talking after the game, saying that the Hawks had their chance. He told the press that the Hawks had blown their chance, and that the Celtics were going back to the Boston Garden to close it out.

"So we came back to Boston for that Game 7, and he and Wilkins were just going at it. They were matching each other basket for basket, and at the end of the game I asked Larry if that was the best he'd ever played. Larry smiled and just said, 'Yep.' I'd never seen anything like it."

After one more season in Boston, Acres was made available for the expansion draft. Orlando quickly snapped him up. He played three seasons in a Magic uniform, before spending parts of the 1992-'93 season in Houston and Washington. Still he considers himself a Boston Celtic. The longtime Lakers fan is now a part of the Celtic family and has nothing but fond memories of his time spent in New England. He appreciates the history of this proud franchise, and remains a big fan of the legendary Red Auerbach.

"Red is a genius and such a great teacher. The thing I found interesting is that you could always smell his cigar before you saw him coming," he recalls with a chuckle. "The cigar—and all that smoke—are the things I'll never forget about him."

Like Red, Acres can't resist teaching. In addition to his full-time gig at Casimir Middle School, he is currently in the sixth year of running the Mark Acres Basketball Camp. The camp runs two weeks every summer, and usually has between 150-200 kids in attendance. It teaches basketball fundamentals, teamwork, and sportsmanship—many of the things that made Acres such a special player himself.

"We really work with them, show them the proper way to play the game, and then we turn them loose and see what they can do."

Whether giving instruction on the court or in the classroom, one thing remains apparent: Mark Acres is in a class by himself.

Where Have You Gone?

RON BONHAM

Wild Life

It has been more than 35 years since he traded basketball hardwood for the hardwood in and around his native Muncie, Indiana, his love affair with the outdoors carrying him far from all those packed NBA arenas and annual championship celebrations with the Boston Celtics. Since retiring from professional basketball as an original member of the ABA's Indiana Pacers, the one-time Mr. Basketball is now the longtime superintendent at Prairie Creek Park, 2,300 acres of fun and recreation for those looking to get away from it all.

"My dad was an outdoors person," says Ron Bonham, still a basketball legend in the Hoosier state. "He more or less raised me on the river. We fished and hunted all the time. He taught me how to appreciate nature, and how to respect the environment."

Now, with an eye on retirement from the parks system, Bonham is more appreciative and respectful than ever. He knows that he is the exception, that rare person who has spent his entire life doing what he loves most, first as a decorated athlete and currently as the chief caretaker at Prairie Creek.

"I've been lucky," he says. "The opportunity to work at Prairie Creek Reservoir came along at the perfect time for me, as I was getting out of basketball, and I've thoroughly enjoyed it. I've been here for 35 years. My

RON BONHAM

**College: Cincinnati '64 | Height: 6'5" | Weight: 200 lbs.
Position: Guard | Years with Celtics: 1964-'65 through 1965-'66**

Notes: Second-round draft choice of the Boston Celtics (the 16th pick overall) in 1964.
Member of two NBA World Championship teams with the Celtics.

wife has been here at this same facility for 34 years. I've had plenty of other opportunities to make double or triple the money that I make here, but, like that old catchphrase, there are some things that money can't buy."

While fortune may not have been in the cards, fame has followed Bonham since his playing days at Muncie Central High School. Known affectionately as the "Blond Bomber" and the "Muncie Mortar," Bonham finished his career as the leading scorer in the history of Indiana high school basketball with 2,023 points. As a senior he averaged 28 points per game. Bonham was twice a first-team All-State player, and in 1960 he was named Mr. Basketball in the state of Indiana.

"That was a great honor," Bonham says. "I was also lucky enough to be named MVP of both the Indiana and Kentucky All-Star games."

Bonham is quick to point out that team goals have always been more important than individual accomplishments.

"We had a lot of talent on our high school team. We were the top-ranked team in the state during my senior year, and we won 29 straight games to reach the state championship. We lost that game. That defeat will always be the biggest disappointment of my life as a basketball player, because we had some phenomenal talent on that team. All five starters would go on to play Division I college basketball."

Bonham had his pick of colleges following his stellar career at Muncie Central. With over 300 scholarship offers on the table, he ultimately decided to follow the path of another Indiana high school legend, Oscar Robertson, to the University of Cincinnati.

"It was a hard decision," says Bonham. "I talked it over with my parents, and we narrowed it down to two schools—Cincinnati and Purdue. Attending a basketball school was important to me. Purdue was known more as a football power, and the University of Cincinnati was a power basketball program. And with Oscar being there—he was a senior in college when I was a senior in high school—I just couldn't pass up the opportunity to play for the Bearcats."

As a freshman, Bonham would watch Cincinnati win the national championship. (At the time, freshmen were not permitted to play varsity sports.) The Bearcats would repeat a year later with Bonham on the court. Denied a championship in high school, he was suddenly on top of the basketball world.

"What a thrill to win it all. You just can't put it into words," says Bonham. "During my freshman season we ran a run-and-shoot offense, but then the coaching situation changed due to health issues. We played at a slower pace, buckled down on defense, and adopted a completely different philosophy toward the game. This was all new to me, because we had played the run-and-shoot in high school. But I can't complain. The end result was well worth it."

The Bearcats were back in the title game after Bonham's junior season, but they were upset by Loyola of Chicago.

"We were ranked No. 1 in the nation," says Bonham, "and we were winning the game handily. We went into our stall with about ten minutes in the game, which we usually didn't do until there were five or six minutes left, and the momentum changed. We threw the ball away, made too many mistakes, and just didn't handle their zone press very well. Loyola came back and forced overtime. We should have had three national championships in a row, but we let it get away from us."

A two-time All-America selection at Cincinnati, Bonham then found himself drafted by Red Auerbach and the Celtics. Upon joining the team in Boston, he had never been so far away from home.

"I don't know how much my phone bill was," he says, laughing. "But I called home several times a week and would talk for hours."

A great athlete, Bonham was nevertheless ill prepared for those grueling training camps ran by Auerbach.

"I was talking to Red on the phone after the draft, and he says, 'Bonham, you're going to be in the best shape of your life.' At the time, I thought I was already in great shape. In high school I worked out six hours a day. In college I kept myself in peak condition. But then I went to Boston, where there were three openings and between 50 and 60 people competing for those spots. After that first day with Auerbach, there were just a handful of people who came back," Bonham recalls. "I can remember Tommy Heinsohn being carried off the floor after that practice because he'd passed out. But that was Auerbach's way. He wanted to see if you really wanted it."

Bonham survived Auerbach's boot camp, making the cut along with fellow rookie Mel Counts. The Celtics roared out of the blocks; their 62 wins that season were a club record, and the club won its seventh consecutive NBA championship. That 1964-'65 season was not without adversity, however, as team founder Walter Brown passed away on September 7, 1964.

"That was my first year coming in, so I didn't get to know Walter that well," he says. "But everything about that franchise was first class: the travel, the hotel accommodations, everything. It spoiled me, because I was on that first Indiana Pacer team when it was in the ABA. It was the exact opposite. We sat in airports all night long, things like that— just a lot of disorganization. That was never the case with the Celtics, and all of the credit goes to Walter Brown."

While Brown may have owned the team and ensured quality travel arrangements, it was Auerbach who handled the contract negotiations with the players.

"Mel Counts and I went in to sign our first contracts," he recalls, laughing, "and we walk into Red's office. Here he was with his feet up on his desk, smoking his cigar, and the smoke was as thick as a cloud. Well, he takes his feet off the desk, grabs two pieces of paper and shoves them at Mel and me. Then he says, 'This ain't a democracy. Here is what you boys are going to get this year.'"

Little did Bonham know that as a rookie he would witness basketball history firsthand. He was watching from the bench as John Havlicek stole the ball from the Philadelphia 76ers in the 1965 Eastern Conference Finals.

"That whole series was a knockdown, drag-out battle," recalls Bonham. "I can remember Bill Russell trying to throw the ball in and hitting the guy wire in the process. We were all going crazy on the sidelines. And for Johnny Havlicek to make that play, that was one of the greatest moments I've ever been part of as a basketball player. And, of course, you had the famous call by Johnny Most. It doesn't get much better than that."

The Celtics dismantled the Lakers 4-1 to secure the team's seventh consecutive title—and eighth overall. While this may have been old hat to players like Bill Russell and Sam Jones, it was a new experience for Bonham.

"Oh boy, what a great thrill. It was such an honor to be a part of something like that. I remember leaving the court after that last game, and the crowd was going wild. Johnny Havlicek and I somehow got off the beaten trail on the way to the locker room, and our warm-up jackets got ripped off our bodies by the fans. Then our jerseys got ripped off. Then I felt someone grab hold of my trunks, and I thought those were going to get ripped off. Finally some security people got around us and led us back to the dressing room. If it weren't for them, we may have lost all of our clothes before we made it back there."

Red Auerbach would bow out the following season with yet another championship, the team's eighth in a row. The starting five had an average age of 31 that season, and many experts felt the team was too old to win again. How were the Celtics able to overcome the age factor to win yet again?

"We were family," he says, "and a very talented one at that. I remember my first year with the team, and Bill Russell didn't speak to any of the rookies or the new guys coming in to compete for a spot on the team. Havlicek and I had been friends all through college, and I asked John about Bill. John said that that's just the way he is. He said that if you make the team, then Bill treats you like one of the family—and that's exactly the way it happened for me. After I made the team it was just like night and day. Russell and his wife would invite us over to their house for dinner, or over to his soul food restaurant in downtown Boston, and he made you feel like a part of the family. So the talent was there, and the love for one another was there. That really made the age factor irrelevant."

After two world championships with the Celtics, Bonham signed with the Pacers of the fledgling ABA. He retired from professional basketball in 1968, and was at Prairie Creek Reservoir less than a year later. Along the way he has served three four-year terms as county commissioner, built a new home on a 60-acre tract of land just east of the reservoir, and opened a kennel for Springer Spaniels.

"Our new home is situated in a state wildlife habitat," he says. "We have an abundance of quail, and we just put in a new six-acre wetland. We travel to North Dakota a couple of times a year to hunt, and vacation in Iowa several times as well. If my health holds out for a couple of more years, then I'm going to retire and ride off into the sunset."

For a man who loves wildlife, it has been a very rich life indeed.

CARLOS CLARK

Making the Cut

His NBA career might have lasted far longer than two years had it not been for several unfair breaks. Yet today, Carlos Clark, at age 45, has no bitterness concerning his experiences during a 13-year basketball career. As a fourth-round draft choice of the Celtics in 1983, Clark was a huge longshot to make the team. However, new Boston coach K.C. Jones liked the six-foot-four guard's defensive abilities and his quickness on the fastbreak. Still, the University of Mississippi lefty didn't see himself surviving the final cuts.

"The Celtics had a ton of veteran guards, all of whom were big names. They had [Danny] Ainge, [Gerald] Henderson, [Quinn] Buckner, [Dennis] Johnson, and M.L. [Carr]. Really, with the exception of Buckner, all the rest of them could play my position, the two guard," Clark says. "Then there was also Charles Bradley, who had been Boston's first-round pick in '81 and a guy named John Schweitz, who was the last guy cut the year before I was drafted. I knew the Celtics liked him a lot. Schweitz and Bradley also played the two spot."

The Boston coaching staff gradually discovered during the exhibition season that Clark had the ability to pressure the ball and force turnovers, which was something Coach Jones was looking for in rounding out his roster. In the final week, Jones released Bradley and then Schweitz, who

AP/WWP

CARLOS CLARK

College: Mississippi '83 | Height: 6'4" | Weight: 210 lbs.
Position: Guard | Years with Celtics: 1983-'84 through 1984-'85

Notes: Fourth-round draft choice of the Boston Celtics in 1983. Won NBA championship as member of the Celtics (1984). Waived on October 22, 1985.

was eventually picked up by Seattle. To his amazement, Clark was officially a Celtic.

"Even during the first week of the season, I was worried the team might pick up some veteran and let me go," recalls Clark. "K.C. must have guessed I was concerned, because he came up to me after a practice and told me, 'Relax, play your game, and go find yourself an apartment, because you've earned a spot here for the season.'"

As the team's 12th man, he saw action in only 31 games his rookie year. His quiet, unassuming nature, combined with his feisty, all-out effort in practice, earned the respect of his teammates. "We wanted to see him get as much playing time as possible," says Robert Parish. "You root for somebody who's a great teammate."

The reward for Clark's work ethic would eventually come in the form of a championship ring. "I keep it locked up. Every once in a while I put it on just to remind myself of how lucky I was to be a part of that great team," he says.

Clark bucked the odds again the following season. Boston had drafted 6'6" swingman Michael Young, starter for the University of Houston's "Phi Slamma Jamma" team, with its first-round pick. Then, in the third round, the Celtics selected skilled Virginia outside shooter Rick Carlisle. Even though the Celtics had dealt guard Gerald Henderson to Seattle, there were seven guards battling for six roster spots. Most of the media predicted that either Clark or Carlisle would be released. Surprisingly, Jones opted instead to waive Young.

"That shocked me," says Clark. "I mean Young was an All-American on a great team. He had guarantees in his contract. I thought he was safe, and Rick and I were on the bubble."

In 62 brief appearances in 1984-'85, the reserve guard averaged 2.7 points on 42-percent shooting. "I got more playing time than my rookie year," Clark says. "K.C. would usually bring me in when we had a lead and he wanted some fresh legs on defense. It's only natural to be frustrated when you're sitting instead of playing. With this team, though, I was just glad to contribute when I could."

In the 1985-'86 preseason, Carlisle won the battle for the final roster spot over Clark. "I saw the writing on the wall pretty early," recalls Clark. "We started with 20 guys in camp, and we split into three teams. When K.C. made the early cuts, we went to two teams. From that point on, I hardly got off the bench in the exhibition games. I knew the coaching staff had just about made their decision."

Before waiving Clark, though, Boston's player personnel director, Jimmy Rodgers, attempted to work out a trade with Chicago in which Clark would become a Bull in exchange for a future draft pick.

"We just wanted to see Carlos playing in the NBA. With his talent and attitude, he could help a team," says Rodgers. "We came close with the Bulls, but the deal fell through at the last minute."

Once Clark cleared waivers, the LaCrosse Catbirds of the CBA, then coached by Flip Saunders, signed him. The guard's efforts in the secondary league were so impressive that Sacramento Kings director of scouting Scotty Sterling called Saunders in December and asked him to get Clark on the first plane to Sacramento. "We want to sign Carlos for the rest of the season," Sterling told Saunders. Within two hours, Clark, excited to get a call-up to the NBA, was at the airport. However, as he waited to board his plane, Clark was paged by Saunders, who had some bad news to share. "Carlos, you're not going to believe this, but [Kings General Manager] Bill Russell called me and reneged on the deal," said Saunders. "He told me he decided not to sign you. That's all he told me. It stinks. All I can say is I'm sorry they did this to you." Russell never called Clark to apologize or even offer an explanation. Confused and disappointed, the guard returned to his LaCrosse apartment and rejoined the Catbirds.

"To this day, I don't know why the Kings changed their minds," he says. "But what could I do, anyhow?"

Clark would get one final crack at making an NBA team during the summer of 1986.

"I was invited to both the Bulls' and Bucks' rookie camps," he says. "Because they both were taking place at the same time, I had to make a choice. I went to Milwaukee's because they had three guards—Sidney Moncrief, Craig Hodges, and Ricky Pierce—who were free agents. I thought at least one or two of them wouldn't be coming back. It was the better opportunity."

However, after a four-day tryout, Clark was cut. No other teams expressed any interest.

"At that point, I actually began wondering if there was something I did in Boston which was so bad that no other NBA teams wanted any part of me," he says. "It also crossed my mind that maybe I was being blackballed. But I couldn't figure out why. Every coach I played for liked me as a person. I was sure about that. All I knew is that I did my best with the Celtics, had played well in the CBA, and had been among the top players in the [World Basketball League]. I was also worried that someone was spreading rumors about me. I can't tell you how much that possibility bothered me, because I've always tried to be a good teammate as well as a good player."

In 1988, Clark decided to play for the Calgary 88's in the WBL, coached by former Bulls assistant Mike Thibeault. "The money was much better than in the CBA. I made $60,000 my first season. That wasn't bad pay for a four-month summer league," says Clark, who was named All-League that year. He would play three more seasons for Calgary, twice earning All-Defensive honors.

Realistically, Clark knew he would never get the opportunity to wear an NBA uniform again. So, when he was offered a six-figure contract with Ghent in Belgium, he decided to head overseas. He would play in Belgium for nine years, making the All-Star team seven times and averaging 26 points a year.

"It was a great experience once I got used to the cultural differences," he says. "The only time I got a little scared was when my team was playing in Zagreb, Yugoslavia. As we were about to enter the arena for our game, myself and the other American player on our team saw three soldiers, all holding machine guns, sitting at an outdoor cafe. The two of us were the only blacks on the team and these soldiers were sort of waving their guns in our direction. We couldn't walk fast enough to get into that arena—and away from them. Outside of that, though, playing in Belgium was tremendous. The fans were very supportive, very friendly."

Clark is currently coaching at Seacrest High School—a small private school—in Naples, Florida.

"A year ago I was doing a clinic, and Larry Bird, who has a summer home here, and Rick Carlisle stopped by," recalls Clark. "They spent time signing autographs with the kids and playing a few games of H-O-R-S-E. It was the highlight of the year for these kids."

Clark, now 45 years old, resides in Naples with his wife, Barbara, and ten-year-old son, Deion, whose most cherished possession is a picture taken of himself and Bird.

Clark hasn't given up on landing a job in the NBA.

"I coached at the Chicago Predraft Camp two years ago," says Clark, who is shy, unassuming, and hardly a self-promoter. "I talked to a lot of coaches and general managers about just becoming a part-time scout or even a volunteer scout. I think I'm pretty good at evaluating talent. All I want is an opportunity to prove I could help a team. I make a lot of phone calls to people around the league. I'm patient, and I'm not going to give up. If I get a chance, I have enough confidence to know I can do a good job."

CHARLIE SCOTT

Family Man

Charlie Scott still looks the part. Whether making appearances on behalf of his current employer, Russell Athletics, or simply making the rounds in his hometown of Atlanta, Scott still looks as if he could take to the court and hang with today's NBA hotshots. Articulate, personable, and equally gracious, he is a throwback only in the sense of how he carries himself in the public eye. You won't find his name on the police blotter, and you won't find him writing tell-all books. Scott is whistle-clean, a devoted family man, and unabashedly loyal to the legendary programs for which he played.

"I bleed Tar Heel blue," he says, without hesitation, "and I'll always be a Celtic at heart. You won't catch me complaining about my basketball career, because things worked out pretty well for me, so I feel very fortunate to have had my career evolve the way it did. To be able to play college ball at North Carolina, and then end up winning a championship with the Boston Celtics, it just doesn't get much better than that."

Twenty-five years removed from his last NBA game, Scott has settled in Atlanta, where he lives with his wife and three children. He spends his days watching his sons play in youth basketball leagues, keeping in touch with old friends like former Celtic teammate JoJo White, and working out to stay lean and trim.

CHARLIE SCOTT

College: North Carolina '70 | Height: 6'6" | Weight: 175 lbs.
Position: Guard | Years with Celtics: 1975-'76 through 1977-'78

Notes: Seventh-round draft choice of the Boston Celtics in 1970. Traded by Phoenix to Boston for Paul Westphal and future draft choices on May 23, 1975. Member of the 1976 NBA champion Celtics. Played in the NBA's "Greatest Game Ever," Game 5 of the 1976 NBA Finals between the Celtics and Suns.

"I eat at Subway," says Scott, laughing, when pressed for his secret to looking so good.

The South seems the perfect fit for the man who attended Laurinburg Academy High School in North Carolina. Described as "an itty-bitty town in the middle of nowhere," there is little else to do in Laurinburg but play basketball. The school has a rich basketball tradition; Chris Washburn, Sam Jones, and Jimmy Walker (Jalen Rose's dad) all played there, and Scott is quick to point out that jazz legend Dizzy Gillespie played the trumpet at Laurinburg before dropping out in 1935. All those memories Scott made in the South—first as a high school standout and later as a two-time All-America selection at North Carolina—provided the motivation for moving his family to Georgia.

"I lived in California from 1980 until 1990," Scott says. "Then I accepted a position with Champion, the athletic apparel company, and moved back to Atlanta. California was nice, but this is home.

"I worked for Champion for seven years as a sports marketing director and then took a consulting position with Russell Athletics," says Scott. "My job is important to me. I enjoy my work. But I'm also focused on my family because, in today's society, a father has to be more involved with his kids. So between helping with their schoolwork and all the extracurricular activities, I've taken a bigger role in their lives. I stay busy, but spending time with my family is very important to me. I really enjoy being with my wife and kids."

Born on December 15, 1948, in Harlem, Scott rarely missed an opportunity to participate in pickup games. He began playing organized basketball at the age of 12. He played bitty-ball first, then AAU ball, and somewhere along the line he fell in love with the game. By age 14 it was apparent that Scott was equally bright in the classroom. He attended New York's prestigious Stuyvesant High School, which specializes in mathematics, science, and technology. Some of the most renowned professionals in the country have attended Stuyvesant, and Scott hardly felt out of place.

But there was a downside.

"They didn't allow me to play on the basketball team," he says. "It was a high standards school, which helped me to prepare academically for life as a collegiate student-athlete. Stuyvesant also helped me to become more responsible."

He transferred to Laurinburg prior to his tenth grade season, and basketball was suddenly back on the radar. Three years later, Scott found himself being recruited by former Maryland coach Lefty Driesell, then the head coach at Davidson College. Practically signed, sealed and delivered, Scott never really thought about playing anywhere else. He got along well with Driesell. He liked the campus. And at the time, Davidson was one of the premier basketball programs in the country.

"My mind was made up," Scott says, "Davidson was the place for me. But my high school coach talked me into looking at all of my options. He used to take me to watch the Tar Heels play. Deep in his heart, I think he wanted me to go to the University of North Carolina, so he was very persistent in making sure that I kept an open mind. And the more I visited the campus, the more I became enthralled with the school.

"As exciting as North Carolina was, it was equally hard to break the news to Lefty. He was the first person who really recognized me, noticed me, and gave me notoriety. I had gone to his basketball camp as a junior in high school, and that's when he offered me a scholarship. He told the world about me—no one had really heard about Charlie Scott before I attended Lefty's camp, but that all changed afterwards. It was the start of a tremendous recruiting circumstance."

Scott's decision to play for the Tar Heels was groundbreaking. He became the first African-American scholarship athlete in the school's history, helping to pave the way for other Carolina greats such as Phil Ford and Michael Jordan.

"It was a different time and place," says Scott. "Back then, African-Americans didn't have a lot of players that they could identify with and cheer for. I was the first in many respects, and it was an honor to represent them the way that I did."

Represent them he did. In addition to being honored twice as an All-American, Scott was All-ACC three times while leading the Tar Heels to two consecutive ACC championships and Final Four berths in 1968 and 1969. Ironically, Scott and Driesell would cross paths once more, this time during the 1969 East Regional final. With a trip to the Final Four at stake, Scott connected on 10 of 14 field goal attempts in the second half, including a 20-footer with three seconds left to eliminate Davidson from the tournament.

"That was a big thrill," he says. "[As was] scoring 40 points against Duke in the ACC tournament was really special. Those are moments I'll never forget. But the biggest thrill I ever had—and I think the biggest thrill that anybody has in that program—is simply being a part of North Carolina basketball. The camaraderie that comes by being there, by being a part of the team, by being part of starting the tradition…I think it's bigger than any one game or one moment. Ask anyone who has played there—Walter Davis, Michael Jordan, James Worthy—and they'll say that their biggest thrill about North Carolina was going to North Carolina."

Scott was also a member of the 1968 United States Olympic Team, where he would team with White en route to winning the gold medal. He was only 18 at the time.

"We were the last team to win the gold medal in consecutive order without any losses. It's a thrill and honor that becomes bigger as the years go on, just as it is to have played for the Tar Heels and the Celtics. I had the best of all worlds when it comes to basketball. I don't think I can be a person who moans and groans about my tradition of basketball and who I played for, and who I played with, and what we accomplished."

Following graduation, Scott was selected by the Virginia Squires of the ABA and the Boston Celtics of the NBA. He chose the former, setting into motion a series of events that ultimately led him to Boston Garden. He played two seasons for the Squires, being named Co-Rookie of the Year following the 1970-'71 season and being honored as an ABA All-Star both years. Although he teamed with a young Julius Erving during the 1971-'72 season, Scott yearned for the NBA stage. He bolted to the Phoenix Suns prior to the start of the 1972-'73 regular season.

Scott's time in Phoenix proved to be a mixed bag; he was an All-Star in three of his four seasons with the team, but the Suns were never serious contenders for an NBA championship.

"It was a great experience," Scott says. "Being in the NBA was everything that I thought it would be. I enjoyed playing in Phoenix, but we didn't have the type of personnel capable of playing against the Jerry Wests, the Wilt Chamberlains, the Willis Reeds, the Walt Fraziers, the Dave DeBusscheres. We just didn't have the personnel to win consistently against some very strong teams. Management was trying its best to improve the situation, but we were only winning 40-plus games a season and only two teams in each division were making the playoffs. So it was a humbling experience. I wanted to make the playoffs, I wanted to succeed at a high level, but we just weren't able to put it together and do the things that I was hoping that we could do."

All of that changed on May 23, 1975, when Boston traded the promising Paul Westphal and two picks to Phoenix for Charlie Scott. The Celtics had won an NBA crown in 1974, and the Scott-Westphal trade put the team on the fast track for yet another title. Suddenly Boston could boast a backcourt of Charlie Scott and JoJo White, easily the best guard combination in the league at that time. Add players like Dave Cowens, John Havlicek, and Paul Silas to the mix, and the Celtics were positively lethal.

"I've always been a Celtics fan," says Scott. "I've always been in love with winning, so I knew that Boston was going to be the perfect fit for me. Red Auerbach is a living legend, a genius, and being able to play with guys like Cowens and Havlicek just made it that much more special."

The team won 54 games that season, before methodically working its way to the 1976 NBA Finals. Ironically, Westphal and the Suns awaited.

"It's funny how that worked out," Scott says, "but we were very confident about our chances of winning the series."

The Celtics would prevail in six games, garnering the team's 13th championship banner. The series is best known for that triple-overtime classic in Game 5, but Scott was dominant in the Game 6 clincher in

Phoenix, with 25 points, 11 rebounds, five steals, and three assists. Scott smiles at the memory.

"I'm going to tell you what I told [columnist] Bob Ryan," he says proudly. "We never worried about Phoenix beating us in that series. People forget that we were up by 25 points in that triple-overtime game, and the Suns were somehow able to come back and force it into overtime. My hat goes off to them for that. It's called the 'Greatest Game Ever,' and I'm glad to be a part of that, and it's great for folklore. But the honest truth is that we were never worried about losing that series. We had beaten them all year long. We looked at it player to player, and we couldn't see where we could be beat. JoJo White versus Paul Westphal: JoJo's going to win that. Me against Ricky Sobers: I'm going to win that. Paul Silas and Garfield Heard: Paul's going to win that. John Havlicek and whoever they're going to put out there on the other end of the court: doesn't matter, because John's going to win that. Same with Cowens. So we knew we were going to win that series. There was no question about that."

The 1976 season marked the highlight of Scott's NBA career. He would play four more seasons, including a brief stint with the Los Angeles Lakers, before retiring as a Denver Nugget. Still, he considers Boston his NBA home.

"We shared a lot of things together as a team," Scott says. "I just enjoyed my whole time there. The friendships mean more than anything. To this day I remain close to JoJo. We get together as often as possible, and talk on the phone all the time. And that just goes back to the Tar Heels and the Celtics being like family. Once you play for these organizations you become a part of the family, and that's the way it will always be."

BAILEY HOWELL

The Natural

He spent his entire athletic career collecting awards—first garnering All-State and All-America honors in high school, then consensus All-America recognition in college, and finally All-Star status in the pros—so it is only fitting that Bailey Howell's name now adorns its own trophy, a rugged likeness of himself awarded annually to the top college basketball player in the state of Mississippi. The Cellular South Howell Trophy made its debut on April 14, 2005, and was awarded to Lawrence Roberts,   a 6' 9" senior center at Mississippi State University. For the modest Howell, the award served as a reminder of how far he had come in his life, from those long days in the cotton fields to the parquet of the Boston Garden.

"I'm very grateful to be recognized in this way," says Howell, ever the gentleman. Retired and living in Starkville, Mississippi, the Hall of Fame legend was on hand for the presentation ceremony in Jackson. "I never dreamed that my name would be associated with something like this. It's a great honor."

"Bailey really is a very genuine person," says Michael Rubenstein, executive director of the Mississippi Sports Hall of Fame & Museum. "He is very humble, but he must have had some deep level of inner toughness to have averaged an unbelievable 20 rebounds a game as he did his senior

AP/WWP

BAILEY HOWELL

College: Mississippi State '59 | Height: 6'7" | Weight: 220 lbs.
Position: Forward | Years with Celtics: 1966-'67 through 1969-'70

Notes: Traded by the Baltimore Bullets for Mel Counts on September 1, 1966. Member
of two NBA championship teams with the Boston Celtics. Enshrined
in the Naismith Memorial Basketball Hall of Fame on September 29, 1997.

year at Mississippi State. It's very appropriate that the award was named after him."

Cast in bronze and walnut and weighing over 40 pounds, it is also fitting that the inaugural Howell Trophy went to Roberts, who like Howell is known for his rebounding prowess.

"Oh, I've seen [Howell's] numbers," said Roberts, who averaged 17 points and 11 rebounds last season. "I've seen the records. They're way up there. Winning the award, and both of us being great rebounders, that's another plus."

Hoops were almost effortless for this human rebounding machine. From the first time he picked up a basketball, Bailey Howell possessed a gift that very quickly set him apart from his peers. He was a natural on the court, at home within its geometric confines, a player so skilled that at the time of his retirement from the NBA in 1971, Howell ranked among the league's top 10 leaders in nine statistical categories. But statistics only tell part of the story. Howell, who grew up near the cotton fields surrounding Middleton, Tennessee, never made himself bigger than the team. Regardless of his star power, he was always willing to subjugate his considerable game for the bigger cause. Such characteristics explain how Howell, a six-time NBA All-Star, blended perfectly with Bill Russell's Boston Celtics, winning two world championships as the curtain closed on arguably the greatest sports dynasty ever.

But it wasn't just natural ability that set Howell apart. It was the strong work ethic, instilled by his parents, which helped to make him special on the basketball court. For Howell, his days were spent working the fields or helping with chores around the family homestead. It was a simpler life back then, with very little in the way of distraction.

"Middleton was a very small town of maybe 300 people or so," says Howell, "and our family actually lived plumb out of the city limits. It was a rural, farming community with no industry to speak about. Tennessee Gas built a pump station there during my teenage years, with lines running from Texas and Louisiana on up into Tennessee. Other than that, the area was mostly made up of farms and small businesses.

"Basketball was the only sport offered at our high school. There were no football or baseball teams for the students, so we'd play pick-up games whenever we could. Our school year started in early August because we would turn out in late September, during the cotton harvest season. Basketball practice didn't start until after we resumed our classes, but we would get together on our own and practice whenever we could.

"We played basketball most of the year. After the regular season was over we would play in the regional and class tournaments, and then we'd play informally through the spring and summer. We only attended school eight months out of the year—we were always out in May, so that we could help chop cotton—so it was important to have a sport to play when we weren't working."

Howell excelled on the hardwood, earning All-State honors in 1954 and 1955. As a senior, he averaged 32.1 points per game.

"Following my senior season, I was selected to play in the annual Murray State High School North-South All-Star Basketball Game. I played well, grabbed a bunch of rebounds, and was selected to the All-American team. They don't play that game anymore, but back then it was one of the most prestigious events in high school basketball."

Following graduation, Howell enrolled at Mississippi State University. There were plenty of other offers, but the raw-boned forward wanted to play in the SEC. Kentucky came calling, as did Tennessee and the University of Mississippi, but MSU proved to be the best fit for the versatile power forward. Like Larry Bird at Indiana State decades later, Howell found himself more comfortable on a smaller campus with a more relaxed atmosphere. And it was at MSU that his virtuosity shone through; in an era when big men were planted firmly around the basket, Howell displayed a guard's shooting touch from the outside. He was a glimpse into the future of basketball, an offensive anomaly, and his presence on the court wreaked havoc on opposing defenses.

As a three-year letter-winner, Howell led MSU to a 61-14 record over three seasons, averaged 27 points per game, and helped the school garner its first ever SEC crown. Back then, freshmen weren't eligible to play on the varsity team, so Howell's coming-out party didn't occur until a year later, when MSU defeated the highly ranked Kentucky Wildcats. Howell torched Rupp's Kentucky Wildcats for 37 points, serving notice that he could excel against the best programs in the country. It was the first Bulldog victory over a UK team in 35 years. As a senior, Howell fulfilled another goal—winning the SEC Championship. "One of the highlights of my career," he says cheerfully.

The two-time consensus All-American graduated from college on time, and with a treasure trove of accomplishments to call his own. Among them: Becoming the first SEC player in history to reach the 2,000-point, 1,000-rebound club; producing a career-high 34 rebound performance against LSU; finishing as the leading scorer and rebounder in MSU history; leading the NCAA in field-goal shooting as a sophomore (.568 in 1957); and capturing two Southeastern Conference MVP awards (1958, 1959).

For Howell, NBA basketball was the next logical progression. Urban legend has it that Cincinnati, choosing first, wanted to snatch the six-foot-seven rebounding machine to bolster its anemic frontcourt. But unable to reach contract terms prior to the draft, Royals management swung a deal with Detroit, allowing them to take Howell with the second overall selection. He was an All-Star by his second season, the first of six such honors. The Pistons, however, struggled in the win column. During Howell's five years in Detroit, the team never finished better than second place in the standings. They were also unable to get past the Lakers and into the Finals. It was a frustrating period in Howell's professional life, but he never complained publicly. Nor did he demand a trade. Instead he played five solid seasons for the Pistons, appearing in at least 75 games per campaign, while averaging more than 20 points and 10 rebounds per game over that span.

Struggling to improve, the Pistons traded Howell to the Baltimore Bullets prior to the 1964-'65 regular season. Howell's two seasons in a Baltimore uniform proved to be even more challenging than the previous five in Detroit; the Bullets struggled despite a talent-laden roster, and the lack of team harmony began to wear on the MSU product. All of that changed on September 1, 1966, when Red Auerbach sent backup center

Mel Counts to Baltimore in exchange for Howell. It was a move that helped rejuvenate both Howell and the aging world champions. Despite having their string of eight consecutive NBA titles snapped by the Philadelphia 76ers, the Celtics benefited immediately from Howell's offensive punch. His contributions factored heavily into the team's championship runs the following two seasons, giving Howell a pair of rings and the perfect capstone to a hall-of-fame career.

Says Howell on joining the Celtics: "It was a big thrill to go from a club with mediocre success to a team that had won eight NBA championships in a row. I got to play with players like Sam Jones, John Havlicek, and Bill Russell, which was very special for me, because they were such special people. The Celtics were the defending champions when I arrived, but they were aging together as a team. The key players were brought in at roughly the same time, and the team always had the last pick in the draft. That made it much harder to bring young guys along, so Red offset this by making trades to improve the team. Willie Naulls is a good example of this. Don Nelson and Wayne Embry played for the Celtics because of Red's shrewdness.

"Mel Counts was a backup center, a seven-footer who couldn't shoot from outside. And because Russell was playing 48 minutes a game, Counts never got the opportunity to play. Red used this to his advantage. He had an unknown commodity, so he built Counts up in the eyes of the Baltimore brass. There was a glut of forwards on the [Bullets] at the time, thanks to a trade with New York, and there wasn't really a center on the roster. Johnny Kerr was at the end of his career, and he was dealing with back problems. Bob Ferry wasn't really big enough to play center. So when the Bullets traded Walt Bellamy to the Knicks just eight games into the 1965-'66 season, the team began to explore trade opportunities. They decided to part with either me or Gus Johnson in order to get their center. It was a big break for me."

In 1967, the Celtics had their streak of eight consecutive NBA championships snapped. Many experts thought that Boston was too old to win another title, but in 1968 that's exactly what happened. For Howell, it was an incredibly satisfying event.

"We won that '68 title by beating the Lakers in six games, the last of which was in Los Angeles," he says in his familiar southern drawl. "That didn't surprise me, because our road record that year was outstanding. We took two of three road games against Detroit in the first round of the playoffs, three of four from Philly in the Eastern Division Finals, and then two of three from the Lakers to win it all. Philly had the best record in the league again, with basically the same club that won the title the year before, and we finished even farther behind them in the standings. But we played better at the most crucial times. We won Game 1, Game 5 and Game 7 in Philly—in our minds, the team that presented the biggest obstacle in winning it all. We were favored to beat the Lakers, and we dominated them.

"The next year Wilt was traded to Los Angeles. [Philadelphia] wasn't the same without him, and we beat the Sixers 4-1 in the opening round. New York was developing a really good club at that time, with players like Willis Reed, Walt Frazier, Dick Barnett, Dave DeBusschere, and Bill Bradley. They were the up-and-coming team, but we beat them head to head and ended up facing the Lakers again in the Finals.

"We barely made the playoffs that season. People often forget that fact. We were 48-34, but we were able to put it together in the playoffs. The Finals against the Lakers was a tough, competitive, hard, monumental struggle. We prevailed, but I remember having no energy left after it was over. I was so tired, but it still felt great because we'd won another championship."

Howell would play one more season, for Philadelphia, finishing his career with averages of 18.7 points and 9.9 rebounds per game. On September 29, 1997, he received basketball's highest honor: enshrinement in the Naismith Memorial Basketball Hall of Fame. Standing at the podium before a large contingent of family and friends, Howell thanked those closest to him as he reflected on a lifetime of hard work and dedication. He displayed the same humility that he'd carried with him since childhood, and then he walked away, a true southern gentleman, proud of his accomplishments but unwilling to make any bigger deal out of them. To those who know Bailey Howell best, his acceptance speech was as genuine as it was natural—a true reflection of the man himself.

"That [hall of fame induction] was icing on the cake for me," Howell says. "Many of my heroes—the people I admired and looked up to—were already in the Hall of Fame, so it was a thrill to join them. I really don't have the words to describe what I felt that night. It was a great evening. I was very proud. Most of my family was there, so it was one of the big highlights of my life. To be recognized in my profession as one of the people who achieved, as one who tried to reach my full potential…it was a very humbling experience. I'll never forget it."

Just as future recipients of the Howell Trophy will never forget what it's like to win such a prestigious award.

TERRY DUEROD

Doing the "DO-O-O-O"

His signing rated nothing more than a sentence in the transactions column. In fact, when Boston signed Terry Duerod to a ten-day contract in December of 1980, the second-year NBA guard knew he might not stick around long enough to have time to unpack his suitcase. After all, the Celtics had a deep backcourt corps, including Tiny Archibald, Gerald Henderson, Chris Ford, and M.L. Carr.

A third-round pick of the Pistons in 1979, Duerod had an outstanding college career at the University of Detroit where he averaged 23.3 points on 53 percent shooting as a senior. In his first NBA season with Detroit, Duerod played solidly, scoring 9.3 points a game on 47-percent accuracy. After being selected by Dallas in the 1980 expansion draft, Duerod was shocked when he was cut just two months into the season.

"I was getting decent [playing] time," recalls Duerod. "My shooting touch was good, and I was fifth on the team in scoring. Next thing I know, they call me in after a practice to tell me they had released me. No one explained why."

Fortunately for Duerod, the Celtics brass, particularly Bill Fitch, liked the 23-year-old's shooter's mentality. As soon as he cleared waivers, Boston signed him. "When I arrived, the first thing Coach told me was

AP/WWP

TERRY DUEROD

College: Detroit '79 | Height: 6'2" | Weight: 180 lbs.
Position: Guard | Years with Celtics: 1980-'81 through 1981-'82

Notes: Drafted by the Detroit Pistons in the third round of the 1979 NBA draft. Signed as a free agent by the Boston Celtics on December 4, 1980.
Waived on October 26, 1982.

that he brought me in because he knew I hit the outside shot," says Duerod. "Basically, he let me know that if I was open and got the ball, he didn't want me to hesitate.

"That talk made me feel pretty good about my chances of sticking. I was realistic, though. I was on a great team. I was the fifth guard, just a second-year guy on a ten-day. No one had to tell me the minutes weren't going to come easy."

Duerod made his Celtics debut in the closing minute of his third game in uniform against the Knicks at Madison Square Garden. On a fastbreak, his lone field goal try, a jumper from the top of the key, rimmed out.

"About the only thing I remember," he says, "was what Larry Bird said to me afterward in the locker room. He told me to take that shot every time."

In the next game, a Boston blowout over Indiana at the Garden, Fitch called on Duerod during garbage time. Once again, the eager-to-please guard found himself wide open beyond the three-point arc. This time he didn't miss. The sellout crowd acknowledged his basket with a burst of applause while the now-resting Celtic starters stood up and yelled out words of encouragement.

After the game, Fitch informed Duerod that the Celtics were going to sign him to a second ten-day contract. In his next few appearances, Duerod played well enough to convince Red Auerbach to offer him a contract for the remainder of the season. The move resulted in the release of guard Wayne Kreklow, who had been placed on the injured list when Duerod first arrived.

It was in mid-January when Duerod put on a garbage-time shooting exhibition against the Nets that would endear him to the Garden crowd for as long as he wore a Celtics uniform. With less than four minutes remaining and Boston safely in front, Fitch looked down toward the end of the bench and motioned for the guard to sub in. Sprinting to the scorer's table, Duerod smiled as several courtside spectators shouted out, "DO-O-O-O." Not more than a minute after entering the game, Duerod came off a pick and buried a mid-range jumper. Two possessions later, he took a pass and flicked in a baseline pull-up. The deep-voiced sounds of "DO-O-O-O" were now becoming much louder. And when he effortlessly dropped in a 20-footer for his third straight basket, the whole building was doing the "DO-O-O-O."

On the Celtics bench, M.L. Carr realized he might be witnessing the birth of a folk hero. "Max, Larry, Chris, myself, we were all standing, waving our arms, and looking up at the crowd," he says. "I mean people were having so much fun. I still remember Larry pointing at Terry and yelling for our guys on the court to get him the ball. And to cap everything off, he got wide open for a three-pointer and nailed it. We're all high-fiveing each other and going, 'DO-O-O-O, DO-O-O-O, DO-O-O-O.'"

When the final buzzer sounded, the somewhat startled reserve headed toward midcourt where most of his teammates formed a spontaneous welcoming line. Hundreds of fans were still at their seats, serenading Duerod with rhythmic chants as he headed to the locker room.

"I guess I was smiling, I don't remember. It was like being in *The Twilight Zone*," he says. "I couldn't believe how the crowd had reacted. I mean it was just garbage time. ...To see and hear everyone cheering for me like that, it was unbelievable, something I'll never forget."

Although Duerod averaged only 2.5 points for the Celtics during the 1980-'81 regular season, fans never failed to salute him when he made his usual late fourth-quarter appearances. "He was the exact type of guy Fitch looked for in an 11th or 12th man, someone who was hard-working, knew his role and got along with everybody," says Gerald Henderson. "Don't get me wrong, Terry had talent and wanted to play as much as anyone, but if he didn't get in, he didn't complain. He'd just keep going all out in practice, staying late to play in our subs versus starters three-on-three or four-on-four games, getting ready for the next game."

Of course, Duerod's proudest moment came when the Celtics captured their 14th world championship by beating the Rockets, 4-2 in the 1981 NBA finals. "Being a part of that team, getting my ring, those are memories I always think about."

In the 1981 draft, the Celtics picked Wyoming's Charles Bradley, a 6-5 guard, in the first round and then took a calculated gamble in the third round by selecting Toronto Blue Jays utility player Danny Ainge, BYU's Wooden Award-winning backcourt star. It appeared Duerod's chance of earning a spot on the Boston roster was nil. However, it took Ainge until early December to resolve a legal battle with Toronto to free him from his baseball obligations and sign with Boston.

"Honestly, when I went to training camp, I expected to be released as soon as Boston was able to sign Danny. The Celtics obviously wanted some size at shooting guard. Charles and Danny were both draft picks. They were going to get guaranteed contracts. They both were three inches taller than me," he says. "Still, I had learned that anything is possible when I got cut by an expansion team and picked up by a team that won an NBA title. "

Duerod, with his determination and enthusiasm, not only made the club, he was kept as insurance by Fitch even after Ainge joined the team. For the final four months of the season, he was "stashed" on injured reserve. "I understood the situation. I would have loved to have been playing instead of watching, but... ," he says, with a knowing smile.

Cut by the Celtics shortly before the start of the 1982-'83 season, Duerod was signed by the Warriors but played only five games before he was released. It was his last NBA stop. He spent a year with the Detroit Spirits of the CBA and then played for Scavolini in the Italian League. He finished his pro career in the Philippines, where he played two years.

"After that, my wife, Rosemary, and I decided to go back to Detroit," Duerod says. "I enjoyed being overseas, but all the travel and cultural differences get to you. It was just time to settle down."

Not surprisingly, Duerod found a challenging and rewarding job, becoming a Detroit firefighter in 1987.

"I'm an engineer," he says proudly. "My job is to drive the truck and then to control the water pressure once we arrive at a fire. I've been in some tough situations, like the time we arrived at an apartment fire and saw people jumping out of windows to escape the flames. You have to react so quickly. There's pressure because our job is to save people's lives and protect their property. It's been a job I loved from the day I started."

At 45, Duerod still plays in the Detroit firefighters basketball league. "My knees are a little worn out, but I still enjoy the competition," he says. "As long as my shot is still going in, I'll manage to gimp my way up and down the court."

RICK WEITZMAN

Looking after "Old Yella"

There's nothing wrong with being a daydream believer. Just ask former Celtic Rick Weitzman. As a senior at Northeastern University in 1967, the 6'2" Brookline native had planned on pursuing a business career after graduating. While the starting Husky guard admits there were moments during practice when he would bury a jumper and fantasize about one day making that same shot after taking a pass from Celtics All-Star Sam Jones, he knew such mental visualizations were mere fantasies.

"In my three years on the varsity I averaged 12 points a game as an undersized shooting guard. I led the team in scoring my junior year, but I knew scouts weren't going to flock to see a guy on a team that played schools like Colby, Clark, WPI, Fairleigh Dickinson, BU, URI, and UNH," Weitzman says. "I had a lot of great moments at Northeastern. Now I was ready to move on to the real world."

Luckily, Red Auerbach saw enough of Weitzman to think he was worth drafting in the tenth round. The Celtics general manager happened to be in the Garden stands when Weitzman scored 24 points against Boston University late in the college season. He also was in attendance when the 21-year-old Husky scored 28 points in a New England all-star game that was held a month before the draft.

Courtesy of Northeastern University

RICK WEITZMAN
(CENTER, NO. 26)

**College: Northeastern '67 | Height: 6'2" | Weight: 175 lbs.
Position: Guard | Years with Celtics: 1967-'68**

Notes: A three-year letter winner at Northeastern, Weitzman was a member of one
NBA World Championship team while with the Boston Celtics in 1968.

Back in the '60s and '70s, it was a Celtic tradition to select local players late in the draft to generate positive publicity and also to fill out Boston's rookie camp roster. The odds of Weitzman even surviving rookie camp were astronomical.

"The Celtics had drafted seven guys ahead of me, including their top pick, Mal Graham, a guard who had a great career at NYU," Weitzman recalls. "They also brought in a couple of free agents. I thought for sure I'd get cut. Luckily, I probably played the best basketball of my life and was invited back to vets camp. I couldn't believe it. Now, though, I had to prove myself against much stronger competition. I mean I was trying to earn a roster spot on a team that had won an NBA championship in eight of the last nine years.

"The first day of camp was something I'll never forget. There I was out on the court with guys like Wayne Embry, Bailey Howell, Don Nelson, Satch Sanders, Sam Jones, John Havlicek, Larry Siegfried, and, of course, [player-coach] Bill Russell. I had grown up idolizing these guys and listening to my neighbor, Johnny Most, rave about their talent, guts, and toughness during every one of his broadcasts. Needless to say, I was a nervous wreck as the practice began. Once we started scrimmaging, though, I relaxed and just played as hard as I could. For some reason I still can't fully explain, I played even better at vets camp than I did in rookie camp."

Still, on the day before the regular-season opener, the Celtics had one more cut to make. After practice, Russell decided to have a two-on-two game amongst the four remaining rookies—Mal Graham, Johnny Jones, Neville Shed, and Weitzman.

"All the veterans stayed to watch. It was the most physical, competitive, emotionally draining two-on-two contest I've ever seen," Weitzman says. "I was banging people around, because if I was going to get cut, I wasn't going down without a fight." The half-hour scrimmage ended when Shed hurt his knee. "Afterward, Russell didn't tell me I had made the team," says Weitzman. "I thought I had made the team, but no one officially said I had. So the next night at the Garden I just walked into the locker room and spotted an empty locker with a uniform hanging up, and just started getting changed."

Weitzman's rookie season brought a lifetime of memories. "I was 21 years old, a teammate of so many All-Stars who had won five, six, seven championship rings," he says. "For me, it was mind-boggling to be on the best team in NBA history."

Throughout the year, the eager-to-please guard was assigned certain off-the-court tasks by the vets. "You know, sort of a hazing-type thing," he says. "For instance, when we were on the road, I had to carry a small, old, ugly yellow gym bag around. 'Old Yella,' as it was called, contained Bill Russell's crumpled, sometimes smelly, uniform. It was my responsibility to air out the uniform and then hang it up so it wouldn't look all wrinkled or stink too much when Russell wore it for the next game.

"One time, I forgot all about 'Old Yella' and Russell's stinky uniform. When he put the uniform on, you could see the steam coming out of his ears. Looking right at me, he yelled, 'Guess who's not getting off the bench tonight?'"

Then there was the time Weitzman was driving into the Garden during a snowstorm and there was a huge accident on the Mystic Bridge. "I was sitting in my car, thinking of how much I was going to get fined for being late to a game when I spotted John Havlicek jogging right past me," he recalls. "I yelled out, 'What are you doing? We're two miles from the Garden.' He told me to pull my car into the emergency lane and just leave it. The two of us then ran all the way to the Garden and actually made it to the Garden on time because the game started late due to the weather. The only guy who didn't make it to the game, which we won, was our coach, Bill Russell. [Red] Auerbach had to coach the entire game. Russell finally showed up ten minutes after the game ended. All Auerbach said to him was that "Coach Russell had better fine his best player for missing the game. And make damn sure it's a steep one."

Weitzman played only 25 games in his first and only season as a Celtic. "But we won a championship, I got a ring, and I even scored four points in the championship game, including the final basket," he says.

"There's tens of thousands of kids who would give anything to have the experiences I enjoyed that one year."

During the 1968 exhibition season, Weitzman injured his knee and was released. He returned to Northeastern to complete his degree and also played part-time for New Haven, coached by former Celtic Gene Conley, in the Eastern League. After graduating, Weitzman taught English at Peabody High for 13 years. He also coached Peabody's basketball team for ten years, compiling a 135-67 record.

"I was really proud of the kids I coached," he says. "Considering I took over a team which had zero wins the previous year, we proved that we could compete with anybody."

In 1980, Most recommended to his radio station general manager that he hire Weitzman to be the color commentator for all the Celtics broadcasts. "I wanted the job badly because Johnny was one guy who encouraged me to pursue basketball from the time I was just a little kid. To work with him, one of the game's legends, was another lucky break," he says. "Fortunately I was able to continue teaching while also broadcasting, because the officials at Peabody were very supportive and understanding. It was hectic and sometimes exhausting—but I loved it."

Weitzman's favorite broadcasting moment came one night when Boston was playing the Bullets in Landover, Maryland. "I asked Jeff Ruland, whom Johnny nicknamed 'McFilthy,' if he would do a five-minute pregame interview with us. Ruland asked if we were 'the guys from Boston.' When I told him we were, he said, 'My mom listens to you guys when you do our games and she says you're horse---.'

"Well, I went back to Johnny and told him about Ruland's remarks. Johnny was totally livid. He opened up our broadcast by delivering a message to McFilthy's mother: 'Mrs. Ruland, if you're listening to this broadcast, you'd better turn off your radio, because you're not going to like what you hear.' I didn't say too much during the game because Johnny went on a tirade against Ruland during each and every stoppage in play."

In 1982, Weitzman gave up his broadcasting job to become a volunteer assistant coach at his alma mater. At the same time, he accepted a part-time scouting position with the Celtics. By 1984, he was a full-time scout of college and CBA players for Boston.

Hard work and long hours paid off for Weitzman when Celtics General Manager Jan Volk promoted him to head scout in 1987. "I set up rookie camp, chose many of the prospects we brought in, and arranged individual workouts for potential draft choices," he says. "I guess I'm most proud of two players I really believed in. The first, of course, was Reggie Lewis. While Reggie wasn't a huge secret around the league, he probably wasn't thought of as a first-round pick because [Northeastern] wasn't a big-time program and he didn't play that well at the Portsmouth Invitational or in the Pizza Hut Classic. But because I had seen him play so often in college, I knew he had all the tools to be an excellent NBA player. The other player I really fought for in our pre-draft meetings was Rick Fox, who had a poor NCAA tournament for UNC. His stock really dropped because of that tournament. Twenty-three teams passed on him before we took him."

In 1997, when Rick Pitino came into power, Weitzman was fired. "I suspected I'd lose my job. New bosses always bring in their own guys," he says. "What bothered me was that Pitino didn't have the courtesy to tell me face to face that I was being let go. Instead, I received a phone call from Rich Pond, Pitino's right-hand man, telling me I was dismissed. Pitino didn't even have the class to call me himself. I had done a lot of draft preparation work. I figured, at the very least, he might want to pick my brain about my thoughts on the draft. ...But I guess he figured he knew all the answers."

His days with the Celtics over, Weitzman was quickly hired by the Cavaliers as a scout. "I knew Rick was a great evaluator of talent and a tireless worker. Honestly, I was surprised when Boston didn't keep him," says the former Cleveland GM, Wayne Embry. "It wasn't just my opinion. Rick had a great reputation around the league."

When Embry was ousted from his Cavs position, and Weitzman again found himself unemployed, Marty Blake, head of the NBA's scouting department, immediately contacted him and offered him a part-time job. In addition, ESPN hired him to handle color commentary for its international audience game of the week.

Then, a year and a half ago, Bernie Bickerstaff, who was about to be named GM of the expansion Charlotte Bobcats, asked Weitzman if he would be interested in a position with the new team. Weitzman jumped at the opportunity. "I'm scouting college and the NBDL. I'm also involved in evaluating players at the posteason tournaments and at our pre-draft individual workouts," he says. "It's a great organization. In fact, it reminds me of how the Celtics ran things when I was there, because there's good people there who know how to work together."

Weitzman and his wife, Carol, reside in the Boston area and have two children, Alyssa and Jennifer.

ROBERT PARISH

Chief Appointment

His list of honors and accolades runs almost as long and as deep as his 21 record-breaking seasons in the NBA. Yet Robert Parish remains as approachable as ever, stoic yet cordial, reserved yet gracious, a down-to-earth living legend with the soulful cool of a jazz player. He is Louisiana born and bred, and yet his basketball legacy—a delicious run that produced some of the biggest hoop moments this side of the Bill Russell Dynasty—will be inextricably linked to the northeast. Voted one of the NBA's 50 Greatest, Parish remained a certifiable star even into the twilight of his career, and the intervening years since his retirement have done nothing to dull the luster of his deeds. On September 5, 2003, Parish produced perhaps his greatest slam dunk of all: induction into the Naismith Memorial Basketball Hall of Fame.

"One of the biggest nights of my life," Parish says from his home in Cornelius, North Carolina.

Today Parish is in his second year as part of the NBA Legends Tour, a league-sponsored tour de force that includes such luminaries as Julius "Dr. J" Erving, Kareem Abdul-Jabbar, Bill Russell, Clyde Drexler, Walt "Clyde" Frazier, Moses Malone, Earl Monroe, Dave Cowens, and George Gervin. The Legends Tour helps promote the NBA through a variety of

John McDorough/Icon SMI

ROBERT PARISH

College: Centenary '76 | Height: 7'0" | Weight: 230 lbs.
Position: Center | Years with Celtics: 1980-'81 through 1993-'94

Notes: Won three NBA Championships with the Boston Celtics (1981, 1984, 1986).
Nine-time NBA All-Star. Holds the NBA record for most seasons played all-time with 21.
Holds the NBA record for most games played with 1,611. Retired with 23,334 points,
then 13th best in history, and 14,715 rebounds, then sixth best in history. Inducted in
the Naismith Memorial Basketball Hall of Fame on September 5, 2003.

high-profile events, including parade stops at Tiffany's in New York, and exhibition basketball games in Beijing, China.

"I didn't do anything those first five years after retirement," he admits, laughing. "I just enjoyed the time off. Then I coached in the USBL for a year, with the Maryland Mustangs. Now I'm involved with the Legends Tour, which has been a lot of fun, and I run a Big Man basketball camp in Sarasota, Florida."

And who better to teach than Parish? He is the NBA record-holder for seasons played (21) and games played (1,611), and is ranked second in playoff appearances (16) and fourth in total playoff games played (184). He also departed with four NBA World Championships, three as a member of the best frontcourt trio in basketball history. Mention Robert Parish, and it isn't long before the names McHale and Bird are appended to the conversation. They are the Holy Trinity of frontcourts, the "Big Three," the engine behind those Celtic powerhouse teams of the 1980s.

Born on August 30, 1953, in Shreveport, Louisiana, Parish's parents were God-fearing people who provided as best they could for their son and insisted that he work hard in the classroom. Segregation and racism were very much alive at this time, yet Robert Sr. and Ada Parish did their best to insulate their four children from such ugliness. As a result, young Robert grew up confident and secure, although he was hardly enamored with the idea of playing basketball. He viewed it as work rather than fun, in part because he placed so much pressure on himself to excel. By junior high school it was apparent to one person, at least, that he had the potential to do special things on the basketball court.

"If I had to pick one person who made the biggest impact on me in regard to basketball," Parish says, "it would have to be my junior high coach, Coleman Kidd. He stayed with me, kept encouraging me, and never let me give up on the game."

With Coleman refusing to let up on his protégée, Parish entered the desegregated world of Woodlawn High School. It was a period of growth, both mentally and physically, and Parish found himself loving a game that he once considered drudgery. He flourished on the court, and seemed to grow taller with each passing day. Woodlawn reached the state finals two straight years with Parish dominating in the paint, garnering a state championship along the way. In 1972, he was named Player of the Year in the state of Louisiana. With nearly 400 scholarship offers to choose from, he decided to play collegiate basketball at tiny Centenary College—a mere six miles away from home.

"My parents were very instrumental in helping me to make a decision on where to go to school," he says. "Centenary College was a very good academic school, which was a big plus. It was also a small school, and that appealed to me for a number of reasons. From a basketball standpoint, I preferred a smaller environment. I didn't want to go to a big program and be compared to all the great players who came before me, like a Lew Alcindor [Kareem Abdul-Jabbar] at UCLA, for example. Playing at Centenary allowed me to carve out my own identity and not get caught up in the comparison game.

"The coaches at Centenary were Larry Little and Rodney Wallace, and they put a lot of emphasis on schoolwork and education. Classes came first, and then basketball, not the other way around. This really impressed my parents. It was also very important to me, because I was the first one in my family to get a college education. And it was close to home."

While Parish continued his metamorphosis into one of the country's best centers, the Centenary basketball program was about to fall on hard times. As a small, independent school with no conference tie-ins, Centenary already faced a myriad of problems, such as recruiting players and scheduling games that didn't require extensive travel. Then, just days after Parish's signing, the NCAA punished the school for various rules violations. The probation would last for four years.

"The NCAA gave us a choice," says Parish. "We were informed of the sanctions, and told that we were free to transfer our eligibility to another college. There were a couple of factors that led me to stay; first, I had just become a father, and I didn't want to move away from my child. That was very important to me. And second, it was a group decision by everyone eligible to transfer. There were six or seven of us. We met and talked about it, and as a group we decided to stay on at Centenary College."

A true student-athlete, Parish worked hard in the classroom and maintained an active social life on campus. He didn't own a car, choosing instead to walk wherever he needed to go. In his free time, he chose to remain focused on the newest member of his family. He made his parents proud by receiving his degree in education. And amid all of this, Parish played extraordinary basketball.

It was a different era then, decades before 24-hour sports coverage, multimillion-dollar endorsement contracts, and recruiting wars that reach down to the junior high level. Parish thrived in virtual obscurity, an unknown to everyone in the nation except those closest to the collegiate basketball scene. He averaged 21.6 points and 16.9 rebounds at Centenary, and was named to *The Sporting News* All-America first team as a senior. He also led the nation in rebounding twice.

The Golden State Warriors wasted little time snapping up Parish with the eighth overall pick in the 1976 NBA draft. Stoic and dignified, the rookie joined a veteran team that had won a championship in 1975. His initial role was that of spectator. But as his rookie season progressed, Parish saw his minutes climb. His coach, Al Attles, kept encouraging Parish to practice hard and wait his turn, this even though the rookie never complained about his place in the rotation. He was unselfish to a fault.

His four years at Golden State were a mixture of promise and disappointment. The team was in decline, as players like Rick Barry were kept past their prime, and young talent such as Jamaal Wilkes and Gus Williams were traded before reaching their full potential. Individually, Parish continued to blossom. He became a starter, and then began to play like one of the premiere centers in the league. By his third season he was averaging 17.2 points and 12.1 rebounds per game.

"It was a good time for me," Parish says of his four years in a Warrior uniform. "It was a learning experience, and I was fortunate to have a mentor in Clifford Ray. He took me under his wing and taught me all about being a professional athlete. He taught me about the professional work ethic, nutrition, and about taking care of myself both physically and mentally. That really made a big difference for me, because all I really had to do was concentrate on basketball."

By 1980 the Warriors were looking to rebuild yet again. The Boston Celtics possessed the top pick in the 1980 NBA draft, two spots ahead of Golden State. Red Auerbach seemed set on drafting Purdue center Joe Barry Carroll, and yet he was hardly convinced that Carroll was the answer to Boston's own championship aspirations. So he shopped the pick. He offered to switch picks with the Warriors, on the condition that Parish was included as part of the trade. Golden State eagerly complied, touching off the single most lopsided trade in NBA history: While Carroll would go on to have a serviceable career with the Warriors, Rockets, Nets, Nuggets, and Suns, it was Auerbach and the Celtics who would reap three NBA championships because of the deal. Along with acquiring Parish, Auerbach would select Minnesota's Kevin McHale with the third overall pick—in Golden State's spot—giving Larry Bird superstar-caliber talent along the frontline.

Just like that, the Big Three was born.

"The first day of training camp was very intense, very focused," Parish recalls. "It was almost like a playoff atmosphere. Every practice was like that. At first I didn't realize that Larry, Kevin, and I would become such a respected frontline; we were all just trying to help the Celtics win a championship. And then, after Dave Cowens retired, it gave me a chance to see that we could be something special. I had fully intended to be Dave's backup. I had no idea that he would step down so abruptly. So once we started playing together, I realized that we could be something special. Each of us had something unique to bring to the table. Larry could score from anywhere, and he was the best passing forward to ever play the game. Kevin had the long arms and the brilliant low-post moves. It all just came together."

With taskmaster Bill Fitch pushing his young charges, the Celtics steamrolled to a 62-20 record and a date with the Philadelphia 76ers in the 1981 Eastern Conference Finals. At stake: A chance to compete for an NBA championship. In an historic series, the Sixers—led by the nonpareil Julius Erving—forged a seemingly insurmountable 3-1 series lead. Yet the Celtics were able to fight their way back, winning three consecutive nail-biters to advance. The poise of Boston's young frontcourt made the difference.

"I have to credit Coach Fitch for not giving up on us, and for helping us to stay determined and focused. He instilled a mental toughness and a physical toughness in us. And even when we were down 3-1, he never let us doubt ourselves. He always preached that we could come back, that it wasn't over until Philadelphia won that fourth game, and that started from Day One in training camp. I believe that that's why we were able to prevail in that series."

The Celtics dispatched the Houston Rockets in the 1981 NBA Finals, winning the team's 14th championship. And while the NBA's most storied franchise was celebrating a rebirth, Parish's deeds that season were being admiringly serenaded by the Boston Garden faithful: Mistaken early on by television announcers as lustful boos, the chants were actually that of "Chief! Chief!"

"Cedric Maxwell nicknamed me 'Chief,' because when I came to the Celtics I was always talking about this movie, *One Flew Over The Cuckoo's Nest*. So Cedric finally saw it, and he said that I had similar characteristics of [the character in the movie named] the Chief, because the Chief had them all fooled. He couldn't talk. He was a mute. And then it turns out that there wasn't anything wrong with the Chief. He was just hanging out there in that mental hospital, relaxing, and taking it easy," recalls Parish with a laugh. "Cedric said that I was stoic like the Chief."

While the Celtics came up short in the two seasons following that championship win over Houston, a four-game sweep at the hands of the Milwaukee Bucks in the 1983 NBA Playoffs was clearly the low point. Auerbach responded with two shrewd moves: He named K.C. Jones as the team's head coach, and he traded for defensive stopper Dennis Johnson.

"DJ fortified our defensive presence on the court," says Parish, "and he gave us a great point guard to replace the retired Tiny Archibald. People don't realize just how talented Dennis Johnson was, because he started his career as an off guard and finished it as a point guard. That's a huge transition, and he did it comfortably.

"I rank K.C. as one of the best coaches to have ever coached in the NBA. He was a great X and O coach, but he was also a great people person as well. He was great at relating to his players. One thing I admired about K.C was that he was always able to make that eighth, ninth, ten, 11th, and 12th guy feel like his opinion was just as important as one of the starters. I feel that that's one of the reasons we were so successful under K.C. He was like Phil Jackson and Chuck Daly in that respect."

The Celtics responded to the coaching change, winning the 1984 NBA championship in thrilling fashion. It was Celtics versus Lakers, East Coast meets West Coast, Bird against Magic. No Finals before or since has lived up to the hype.

"I was matched up against Kareem," Parish remembers, "and Kareem is the best player I've ever had to play against, period. No one was ever able to devise a defense to stop Kareem. He exploited every defense that was ever thrown at him. He was smart. He was intelligent. He was an extremely gifted athlete, and the only player I'd ever played against that I could never change his shot. That hook shot was automatic. He shot it the same way every time. Wilt Chamberlain was the only person who ever forced him to alter it. Fortunately, I was able to play him well enough to help us win that series."

The Celtics won it all again in 1986, with the addition of Bill Walton making this team arguably the greatest in NBA history.

"The 1986 Boston Celtics should be ranked as one of the best teams of all time," Parish says. "Easily in the top five, in my opinion. Bill brought toughness to the team, and a knowledge of what it takes to win an NBA championship. He was a part of that championship team with the Portland Trail Blazers, a former MVP, the best passing big man to ever play the game, and he brought great humility to the second unit. He was willing to put his ego aside for the good of the team. How many athletes of his stature are willing to take a lesser role in order to make the team better? I had always respected Bill and admired him from afar because of the way he played the game on both ends of the court. That's how I prided myself. I worked on being consistent and multifaceted, and not just a one-dimensional player. That's the way that Bill Walton played the game."

The Celtics began a slow descent following that championship season, touched off by the tragic death of Len Bias just two days after the 1986 NBA draft. The Big Three were forced to play major minutes, and this began to take its toll; by the early nineties, Bird, McHale, and Parish were shells of their former All-Star selves. Bird would retire first, followed closely by McHale, but Parish would hold up better than any other player in NBA history. He would play briefly for the Charlotte Hornets and Chicago Bulls, before retiring following the 1996-97 season. Twenty-one seasons of stellar play, and through it all, Parish remained a Boston Celtic at heart.

"I will always treasure my time in Boston," he says. "All of the hard work, the championships, everything. And I'll never forget people like the late Johnny Most. He was a chain smoker, and I remember Danny Ainge and Kevin replacing his cigarettes with those exploding party poppers. Johnny would light one up, it would go off in his face, and then he'd grab another one. He went through four or five before he realized what the guys had done, and then he went on a swearing rampage. It was so funny. I can't remember ever laughing that hard."

As Parish travels to promote the league, he certainly has much to smile about. Few players in any sport have accomplished as much as the player known affectionately as Chief. He is a legend, but he remains the same dignified person who grew up humbly in Shreveport, honoring his parents while striving to make his mark in the world of professional basketball.

Where Have You Gone?

RICK ROBEY

The Bruiser

H is name is the answer to one of the most frequently asked Celtics trivia questions: Whom did Boston general manager Red Auerbach give up in order to obtain defensive stopper Dennis Johnson from the Suns?

While Rick Robey would be remembered as the trade bait the Celtics used to snatch Johnson away from Phoenix in '83, the 6'11" center-power forward was hardly regarded around the NBA as "chopped liver." In fact, at the time of the DJ deal, Robey had enjoyed considerable success throughout both his college and pro careers.

As a starter for the University of Kentucky, Robey's inside presence helped lead the Wildcats to the 1978 NCAA championship. In the 94-88 title game win over Duke, the 235-pound All-America big man dominated the lane by hitting eight-of-11 shots, scoring 20 points and grabbing 11 rebounds. "We had a great bunch of guys," Robey says. "Our two main scorers, [small forward] Jack Givens and [guard] Kyle Macy, were pro material. When they did miss, [center] Mike Phillips and I were underneath for the rebounds. From the starters right on down the bench, we just had perfect chemistry, very similar to the Celtics teams I played on."

RICK ROBEY

College: Kentucky '78 | Height: 6'11" | Weight: 235 lbs.
Position: Center | Years with Celtics: 1978-'79 through 1982-'83

Notes: Traded by the Indiana Pacers to the Boston Celtics for Billy Knight on January 16, 1979. Member of one NBA championship team while with the Boston Celtics (1981). Traded to the Phoenix Suns for Dennis Johnson on June 27, 1983.

Chosen third overall in the 1978 draft by the Pacers, Robey, in a backup role to veteran center James Edwards, saw limited playing time during his first three months as a pro. "I was a little frustrated with how I was being used," he says. "But then, right after a Celtics-Pacers game, [Boston player-coach] Dave Cowens walked up to me as we were leaving the court and tipped me off that Red Auerbach was trying to trade for me. I could've hugged him when he clued me in, because I had always dreamed of playing for Boston."

On January 16, 1979, the Celtics did indeed acquire Robey, sending veteran swingman Billy Knight to Indiana. The first year was a learning experience for both the ex-UK big man and the team itself.

"Personally, I got an education every day at practice because I had to go up against Cowens," he explains. "Dave was something else, man. He always played aggressively and very physically, even against his own teammates. He loved contact; so did I. I learned a lot of little tricks from him that first year. I had more bumps and bruises from working against Dave than I got playing in games.

"But the team was really struggling when I got to Boston. Outside of Cedric [Maxwell], [guard] Jeff Judkins and me, everyone else had at least five years' experience. Plus, there were a ton of roster changes throughout the season. Dave was doing the best he could as the coach, but things were just too crazy. One month he'd be worried about how to handle Marvin Barnes or Curtis Rowe, and the next he'd be trying to figure out what to do with Bob McAdoo. I knew from the start that Red was going to clean house. When the season finally ended, everyone knew Dave wanted to just be a player, not a coach."

Despite the fact that Boston ended up with a pathetic 29-53 record and finished dead last in the Atlantic Division, Robey was confident the team could reverse its fortunes practically overnight. The reason for his optimism boiled down to two words: Larry Bird.

"I had never met the guy, but I had sure seen enough of him on TV to know how great he would be as a pro," Robey recalls. "I knew he was pretty cocky on the court—and for good reason. I had absolutely no idea what kind of person he was. It sort of amazed me that it took only a couple of weeks for us to become real good friends. We both golfed and we both enjoyed downing some cold Miller Lites after golf. Before our first training camp together ended, we were drinking buddies. ...Right off the bat, we'd joke with each other non-stop. I'd kid Larry about being drafted two spots ahead of him in the '78 draft, and he'd come right back and go at me about the extra four years of pro experience I got while playing at Kentucky. It was like we knew each other since we were kids."

In Bird's first year, the Celtics, under their new coach, Bill Fitch, enjoyed the greatest one-year turnaround in NBA history, finishing with the regular season with a 61-21 league-best record. Although beaten by Philadelphia, 4-1, in the Eastern Conference finals, Boston clearly was a title contender once again. As the backup for both Cowens and Maxwell, Robey was a key contributor. Playing 18 minutes a game, he averaged 11.5 points and 6.5 rebounds while shooting 52 percent from the field.

Following their elimination by the 76ers, the Celtics made a major move, acquiring veteran center Robert Parish and the third pick of the '80 draft for the second and 13th selections, which turned out to be center Joe Barry Carroll and power forward Rickey Brown. Boston then chose wide-shouldered, long-armed Kevin McHale, a 6'10" power forward from Minnesota, with the pick it had received from the Warriors.

"I knew Robert was a quality player, a guy with a soft jumper who could rebound and block shots. ...[But] the first time I saw him at training camp, I thought he looked sort of awkward," Robey says. "Then, after just one practice, I knew exactly how much this McHale kid was going to help."

The 1980-'81 season turned out to be the highlight of Robey's career. "I played mostly backup center," he says. "Fitch wanted me to play physically, to lean on guys like [Daryl] Dawkins, [Wes] Unseld, and [Bill] Cartwright. My job was to soften them up a little so Robert could run them into the ground. For me, that was fun.

"With Kevin, Larry, and Max rotating at the forward spots and Robert sprinting up and down the court, we'd get out to a lead, and teams would just give up. It was like we were messing with their minds, especially with Larry and Kevin talking trash all the time."

Boston won 62 games in the regular season but had to sweat out a tough seven-game playoff series against Philly to reach the NBA finals. "We were up against Houston and Moses Malone, the league's best rebounder. He was an absolute animal," Robey remembers. "All Fitch told me before the first game was to do whatever was necessary to keep Malone away from the basket. 'I need you to give me at least 15 strong minutes. Push him, bump him, shove him, tackle him. Just don't let Malone get position on you,' Bill told me. 'And one more thing: don't foul out.'

"I didn't, either. We beat them in six games, and I must have picked up 24 [actually 21] personals in the series. I remember Robert kidding me all the time about being a butcher. I didn't mind, because I could see that Malone was getting frustrated. There were a couple times that I hacked him so hard that I swear he was close to slugging me. I loved that because I knew I was doing what Fitch wanted from me."

Robey would play two more seasons with Boston. "My minutes went way down, because both Fitch and then K.C. [Jones] were using McHale to play not only power forward but also at center to back up Parish. By the end of the 1982-'83 season, I saw the handwriting on the wall," Robey says. "K.C., who not only was my coach but a great friend, called me to let me know I was being traded to Phoenix for D.J. I think K.C. expected me to be upset, but I wasn't. I just told him, 'Look, I'd make that deal myself. You're getting the league's best defensive guard.'"

As a Sun, Robey experienced nothing but frustration. "I would have gotten a chance to start, a chance to play a lot of minutes," he says. "From the start, though, I had one injury after another. I had a bum knee my first year. I only played four games my second year there because of chronic pain in my right Achilles tendon. Finally my hip went. I mean I had trouble walking. At the end of the 1985-'86 season, I retired."

Despite the injuries, Robey, who underwent a total hip replacement in 1994, has no regrets. "The Suns were great to me," he notes. "No complaints at all. It just didn't work out the way I wanted."

In 1987, Robey opened a restaurant in Lexington, Kentucky. "The food was excellent, and we were packing the place. The first six months were very successful," he says. "Then, it became obvious that money was disappearing. I was so disappointed that I decided to just close the doors for good."

Moving to Louisville, Robey became a licensed real estate agent. "I was fortunate to learn a lot about the business from two great partners," he says. "We opened up a RE/MAX office and worked long hours to make the business grow. Today we're the top RE/MAX firm in the region, which includes all of Kentucky."

Among Robey's clients: horse trainer D. Wayne Lukas and former Celtics coach Rick Pitino. "They're good friends of mine," he says. "Wayne and I owned a horse together and might buy a couple more."

In his spare time, the ex-Celtic enjoys golfing (an eight handicap) and attending the annual Kentucky Derby weekend. He and his wife, Bonnie, have a 14-year-old son, Sam, and reside in Louisville.

PAUL WESTPHAL

West Side Story

I knew that Paul Westphal was special long before I ever had the pleasure of speaking with him about his basketball successes, of which there are many. The year was 1989, and I caught a television news report that the Phoenix Suns were going to retire Westphal's jersey to their 'Ring of Honor'. Westphal, of course, played his first three NBA seasons with the Boston Celtics, winning a championship in 1974 while studiously preparing to crack Team Green's starting lineup. I'd always admired Westphal—or Westy, as he is affectionately known to legions of fans—so I decided to keep tabs on his special day, knowing full well that his number 44 would have been raised to the Boston Garden rafters had he remained a Celtic.

At some point following the retirement ceremony, I learned that Jerry Colangelo, the Suns' longtime owner, had offered to lavish Westphal with gifts befitting his newly minted status of Official Phoenix Suns Legend. Westphal graciously declined, asking Colangelo to instead donate money to start an education fund with the Christian Family Care Agency, in the name of Armin Westphal, his late father. That stuck with me. In a world run amok with athletes who've lost touch with reality, Westphal was a clean and refreshing breath of fresh air.

PAUL WESTPHAL

**College: Southern California '72 | Height: 6'4" | Weight: 195 lbs.
Position: Guard | Years with Celtics: 1972-'73 through 1974-'75**

Notes: First-round draft choice of the Boston Celtics. Member of the Celtics' 1973-'74 championship team. Traded with future draft choices to Phoenix for Charlie Scott on May 23, 1975.

Fast-forward to the present. I have a date to interview Westphal, but I'm not sure whether he'll remember my name or that we're supposed to talk. He's a busy man, the head basketball coach at Pepperdine University, and fresh off an extended recruiting trip in Europe. And on top of that, the Malibu-based school for which he works is now back in session.

My fears are allayed moments later, as Westphal points out that he's been expecting me. He is kind, courteous, and unpretentious—all of the things that I'd imagined him to be—and he is happy to share stories of his brief-but-eventful tenure with the Celtics, his successful career as both NBA player and coach, and his current gig as the coaching *jefe* at Pepperdine.

"Coaching at Pepperdine is an honor," Westphal says of the post he's held since 2001. "The University's basketball tradition is outstanding. I'm happy with the environment here and with the opportunity that the school provides. I enjoy my job. Athletes who come here get a great education, have a wonderful place to live, and experience great basketball."

While Westphal is clearly happy at Pepperdine, his name has been linked to other NBA openings—and one very high-profile job in particular. In 2004, he found himself on a short list in connection with the then-vacant Boston Celtics head coaching job. President of basketball operations Danny Ainge ultimately settled on Doc Rivers, but not without giving serious consideration to Westphal.

"The Celtics job was pretty close to happening," he says, "and it would be a lie to say that I wouldn't take it if they had offered it. I'd have taken it, no question."

Westphal's passion for hoops is well known and dates back to his childhood in Redondo Beach, California. Born in 1950, Westphal got his first taste of the game in the family's backyard.

"I grew up playing basketball at a very early age, and I was fortunate to have an older brother who played ball with me in our backyard. At the time I was a little guy who just wanted to join in the fun, and I would cry if I didn't get to play," he recalls, laughing. "My brother and my father both taught me a great deal about the game. I often found myself playing against older kids, which meant that they were usually bigger and stronger, and I benefited greatly from those experiences. It certainly furthered my development as a basketball player, both from a fundamentals standpoint and a confidence standpoint. My dribbling and ball-handling skills improved tremendously."

Westphal's prodigious basketball talent blossomed in high school. Starring for Redondo Beach's Aviation High as a senior, he was named CIF "Player of the Year" after averaging 32.5 points a game. He still values his time there.

"Redondo Beach was pretty much a bubble," says Westphal, reflecting on the social and political climate of the 1960s. "And in many respects we really weren't affected by the turbulence of the times. It was a great place to grow up. There was no tension in our neighborhood, and you could go outside and play without fear. It was a great childhood—I rode my bike everywhere, played baseball, you name it.

"My father was an aeronautical engineer and very much devoted to his family. We had a comfortable lifestyle. We weren't rich by any means, but we didn't have to scratch, either. It wasn't a hard existence. We had everything we needed, really.

"Basketball allowed me to travel quite a bit, and somewhere during this period I gained a reputation for being a pretty good player. I was just as comfortable going up against the inner-city kids from Compton as I was the competition in Redondo Beach. I took great pride in my ability to excel in these environments."

Westphal was so good, in fact, that he was sought after by numerous Division I schools. He settled on the University of Southern California, which produced another Celtic great in Bill Sharman. Westphal was a three-time All-Pacific 8 Conference performer at USC, and also a two-time All-America honoree. As a junior, USC compiled a 24-2 record during the 1970-'71 campaign, with the only two losses being to crosstown rival UCLA. To this day he reveres UCLA's legendary coach, John Wooden.

"Coach Wooden is the greatest collegiate basketball coach the game has ever known," Westphal says admiringly. "Red Auerbach holds the same distinction at the professional level."

Did he borrow anything from either of these legendary coaches?

"Although I didn't play for either of them, I certainly feel that I've studied under both of these great men. They are so different and yet so very much the same. Both were obviously influenced by their environments, with Coach Wooden living out west and Red being born and raised in New York. But at the core, both have so much in common, especially basketball-wise. Both understand the importance of playing unselfish, team-oriented basketball, and both have that rare ability to cut directly to what matters most in a given situation."

Westphal was selected in the first round of the 1972 NBA Draft, with the 10th pick overall, by the Boston Celtics. In today's NBA, that would have made him a lottery selection—not to mention an instant millionaire. The draft has changed dramatically since then.

"The most obvious and visible difference is television," Westphal says. "Today's draft is a feature event with extensive media coverage, whereas in '72 it might be covered by radio, the evening news, or page seven of the next day's newspaper. It just wasn't such a big production back then. Another difference is the immediacy of today's draft. I didn't realize who drafted me until Mary Whelan, who was Red's secretary at the time, called to tell me that I'd been chosen by the Celtics. Back then, players received telegrams letting them know which team had chosen them. My telegram was delivered to the wrong destination—Southern California College instead of USC—so I didn't actually receive mine until two days later.

"As for the draft itself, I had absolutely no idea where I'd end up being taken. I'd injured my knee during my senior year at USC and missed the second half of the season, and that made it difficult to figure out where I'd go. I felt that I could have been anywhere from the top two or three players selected to not being drafted at all. Because of my knee, the Celtics took a big chance on me. They had no idea whether it would be sound enough to withstand the rigors of NBA basketball, and that made their selection somewhat of a gamble."

Another big difference is the training camps. Westphal vividly remembers his first.

"Today it can take an NBA player up to three days just to pass a physical. Why? Because the monetary concerns dictate that teams be much more thorough when it comes to a player's health. When I played, I took my physical a full ten minutes before the first practice," he says with a chuckle. "There was a doctor on a stool in the locker room, and his examination wasn't much more than a simple turn-of-the-head-and-cough.

"I remember playing outdoors, on asphalt—that stands out in my mind because of my knee. We practiced at Camp Milbrook in Marshfield, Massachusetts. Red wasn't the coach, but he was always there. We would practice defense for an hour in the mornings, and then follow that with an hour-long scrimmage. The afternoon session was focused primarily on the offense, so we'd run through our offensive sets for an hour and then go straight into another scrimmage. It was hard. There were times when we'd practice to the point of exhaustion.

"The Celtics had a great system in place for bringing along young players. The coaching staff didn't yell at the young guys, so they weren't scared or afraid to make a mistake. It was a very educational experience, and one that was helpful in my development as a professional basketball player."

The Celtics, coached by Tommy Heinsohn, won 68 games during his rookie season, still a team record. It would prove to be a bittersweet accomplishment, however, as Boston was defeated by the Knicks in the Easter Conference Finals. And while Westphal didn't play much as a rookie—the team was loaded with talented players such as Dave Cowens, John Havlicek, and JoJo White—it was clear to everyone that he was going to be a star. He was young and athletic, with a take-it-to-the-basket mentality. And while there were the obvious comparisons to Jerry West, Westphal patterned his game after another player with Laker roots.

"I admired Jerry," he admits, "and early on people often compared the two of us. I guess part of it was because we were both white, but our games were quite dissimilar prior to my knee injury. Jerry was a guard in the classic sense—he had that beautiful, pure jump shot—whereas I was more apt to drive to the basket. So from a physical standpoint I had a resemblance to Jerry, but from an aesthetic standpoint I more closely resembled Elgin Baylor. And to a large degree I modeled my game after Baylor. He had that one-legged jumper, which became a part of my game, and he drove the basketball much more than Jerry did. I emulated him. I would go into the paint and create, sometimes throwing up those crazy shots like Baylor. After the knee injury, I altered my style of play somewhat, becoming more of the traditional perimeter player like Jerry."

By the end of Westphal's second season, the Boston Celtics were once again champions of the NBA. It was the first title without the great Bill Russell. The 1974 NBA Finals provided no shortage of intriguing matchups, including the battle between Dave Cowens and Kareem Abdul-Jabbar. The Boston-Milwaukee series was also notable for its homecourt "disadvantage;" five of the seven games, including the Game 7 clincher in Milwaukee, were won by the visiting team.

"It looked like we'd win the series in six games," Westphal says. "We were up at home when Kareem hit the skyhook from the corner as time ran out. I remember it well because it happened right in front of me; I was watching from the bench! The whole series was memorable and for a number of reasons. The home team clearly didn't have an advantage, and I believe that was because of the incredible adjustments made by both coaches. That series was one of the best examples of counter-punching I've ever seen. To win it, to beat Oscar Robertson and Kareem for the title…that was just a special feeling. Incredible. And I was so young that I thought it would always be like that."

The Celtics failed to repeat as champions the following season, prompting Red Auerbach to make changes. The most significant: trading a hot, young talent like Westphal to Phoenix for an experienced scoring threat in Charlie Scott. It was the rare transaction that benefited both teams, setting both clubs on a collision course in the 1976 NBA Finals.

That Celtics-Suns series will forever be known for Game 5, dubbed the "Greatest Game Ever" by many in the league. Boston prevailed in three overtimes, and then went on win its 13th championship one game later.

Does Westphal have any memories of that triple-overtime thriller?

"There are so many memories from that game, which makes it very hard to pick one thing. When I look back, I think about all of the little things that we could have done differently to win that game. I suppose that's the coach in me. There's nothing you can do to change the outcome—that's basketball—but it still hurt to lose that game and the series as well. As time has passed, I've come to realize what a privilege and an honor it was to be a part of something that special, regardless of which side you were on. That's the thing that stands out most now, and the losing pales in comparison to the bigger picture of what we accomplished in that series."

Westphal would go on to post five consecutive All-Star seasons, four with the Suns and one with the Sonics, before departing for the New York Knicks. He would damage his knee that first season in New York, and earn the NBA's Comeback Player of the Year award the following season. Retiring as a Sun a year later, Westphal embarked on the coaching career that has led him to Pepperdine. This included the exciting 1992 NBA Finals between the Suns and the Chicago Bulls. And while his stop in Boston may have been brief, Westphal will always consider himself a Celtic at heart.

"Red used to say, 'once a Celtic, always a Celtic'," says Westphal. "He preached family and what it was like to be a part of the Celtic Mystique. He was a special person, and I learned a lot from him. Seriously, there is no exaggerating how good Red was when it came to basketball. The man was a true genius. He built the Celtics into champions three different times and is responsible for all 16 banners. You don't do that by accident. A lot of his critics like to say that Bill Russell was the reason for Red's success, but I don't agree with that assessment. Red understood that you had to be lucky—the trade that landed Russell is a perfect example—but he also made the most out of the opportunities that came his way. So to say that Russell was the sole reason for his success isn't a valid argument. He had a gift. He was a winner before Russell, and he was a winner after Russell was gone.

"There is another misconception about Red—that he was hard to play for. In fact it was quite the opposite. When people think of Red they tend to think of him screaming his head off, but Red really didn't scream at his players. He saved all of that for the poor referees. He was a great teacher, and he knew how to treat his players. He supported them.

"When I was with the Celtics, Red would somehow always make his way over to me and share something he noticed during a game. Maybe something was wrong with my shot, or the way I dribbled or defended. Whatever the case, Red would always seem to join me at an adjoining urinal as I waited for a shower, and he would tell me one thing that I needed to work on during the next practice. I learned so much from him during my career with the Celtics."

And now, as the head coach at Pepperdine University, Westphal does his part to pass on lessons learned. A devout Christian, he also keeps his accomplishments in the proper context.

"Basketball has been a huge part of my life, and it has given me so much in this world. It is a large part of who I am. The important thing for me is to keep it all in perspective. I would trade it all away rather than lose touch with what matters most: God and family.

"My advice would be to remember that there is no ultimate victory in this life, and that you have to find out what really matters most—and that true success occurs only after you establish a solid relationship with God."

XAVIER
McDANIEL

The X Factor

The Seattle Supersonics had the fourth overall selection in the 1985 NBA Draft, and with it they hoped to lay the foundation for a championship contender. It was the first year of the draft lottery, and while Patrick Ewing was the obvious overall choice, going to the New York Knicks and taking a giant bite out of the Big Apple, everything else that followed was wide open. With Wayman Tisdale and Benoit Benjamin going to the Pacers and Clippers, respectively, the Sonics wasted little time snatching up the first player in collegiate history to lead the nation in scoring and rebounding in the same season.

That player was Xavier McDaniel, and over the next several seasons the player known as "X" and "X-Man" did indeed become a part of the Sonics' playoff foundation. Today, McDaniel is involved in laying foundations of his own. The owner of "34 X-Man, LLC," this one-time Boston Celtic buys undeveloped property in Columbia, South Carolina, subdivides it into lots, and then builds homes on them from the ground up.

"After basketball I pretty much chilled," McDaniel says, explaining his lifestyle in the weeks and months following retirement from the NBA. "My first few years I lived off what I made. Ask anyone who knows me, and they'll tell you that I take care of my money.

AP/WWP

XAVIER McDANIEL

College: Wichita State '85 | Height: 6'7" | Weight: 232 lbs.
Position: Forward | Years with Celtics: 1992-'93 through 1994-'95

Notes: Signed by the Boston Celtics as a free agent on September 10, 1992 to replace the retired Larry Bird. Played three seasons with the Celtics.

"Ask Robert Parish," he continues, laughing, "and he'll roll his eyes and say 'McDaniel—that cheap bastard!'"

That frugality, combined with a keen business sense and a strong work ethic, has helped McDaniel turn his dream into reality—or, in this case, realty.

"I got started with a friend. We would buy existing homes, fix them up and resell them. A few years later I branched out on my own, and now I'm building homes from scratch. I've been doing that for about nine months. I've already got one house up, and two more that are 95 percent done. I've got three more under construction, and out of those one has already been sold. So I figure I'll do that another eight years, when I can retire again," he says with a laugh. "Then I can start collecting that little NBA pension they give us."

The oldest of six children, McDaniel started playing basketball for the Ben Arnold's Boys Club in Columbia. He was a seventh grader at the time, and by the end of the season he was the league's MVP. Interestingly enough, hoops wasn't his first love.

"I played baseball and football from the age of eight," he says. "In the state of South Carolina, you either play one or the other. Basketball was just something to do in my spare time."

Only 5'10" in the eighth grade, McDaniel was years away from developing the intimidating persona that worked so well for him in the NBA. It is hard to imagine an adolescent X-Man, complete with Afro, but that was Xavier McDaniel circa 1976. He continued to play baseball and football, while finding time to indulge himself in the hobby that would later bring him fame and earn him millions.

"I grew from 5'10" to 6'7" in high school," he says of his development into cage intimidator. "I went through some hard times in high school, not doing my schoolwork, not doing the things necessary to be a student-athlete, and I thank God that I had a very good high school basketball coach. He could have been one of those coaches who did anything to keep his players eligible, but he told me that if I wanted to play on the team, I had to do my schoolwork. I played scrub minutes in the beginning, and I was a starter as a sophomore. I came back for my senior season mad, because I knew I should have been a starter, I knew I should have been on the All-Area team, because at 15 years old I was already a star in Columbia, South Carolina. I didn't play my junior season, but that motivated me. I came back and had one of the best senior seasons anyone in the state had ever put up."

Fueled by that anger, McDaniel led A.C. Flora High School to a state championship. He was the star on a team that produced four Division I college players, including Tyrone Corbin, who would go on to play for nine NBA teams in 16 seasons. "X" averaged 18.8 points and 14.4 rebounds for the A.C. Flora blowout juggernaut, while logging barely more than two quarters per game. His dream of playing at South Carolina seemed like a mere formality at that point, or at least until McDaniel opened the newspaper and was met with disappointment.

"I saw where the school had signed six guys," he says, "and they didn't have any more scholarships. They wanted me to go to prep school, so I decided to look elsewhere. I went to Clemson, Memphis State, and Wichita State on recruiting trips. I had a great time at Memphis State, so that made it hard as far as making my decision. I kept flip-flopping between Memphis and Wichita. I finally told myself I'd sleep on it and pick one the next morning. And I did. I woke up, and told my brother that I was going to Kansas."

The decision proved to be a wise one. McDaniel had a stellar collegiate career at Wichita State, becoming the first player in NCAA history to lead the nation in both scoring and rebounding in the same season. Only two others—Hank Gathers of Loyola Marymount and Kurt Thomas of Texas Christian University—have done so since. He also led the nation in rebounding twice, and in the process was named a consensus All-American. By the time his college career was over, McDaniel had elevated himself into an NBA lottery selection.

"I enjoyed my career at Wichita Sate. I know I made history with the scoring titles, but it never meant a lot because I never won the NCAA championship. At the time I was one of 46 players to score 2,000 points. I grabbed more than 1,300 rebounds—I don't know where I stand now, but at the time that put me second on the all-time list behind Wes Unseld.

But I didn't win a championship. Individuals goals are okay, but team goals were always more important to me."

With the exception of the first choice, the inaugural NBA Draft was rife with suspense. There was plenty of talent, but few can't-miss projections beyond Patrick Ewing. Karl Malone was taken with the 13th pick, behind such names as Jon Koncak, Joe Kleine, and Kenny Green. McDaniel arrived at Madison Square Garden wide-eyed and nervous, unsure as to when his name would be called. He watched as Ewing made his way to the podium to shake Commissioner Stern's hand, followed in short order by Wayman Tisdale and Benoit Benjamin, and then he began to feel a tremendous sense of anxiety.

"We were sitting in a line," McDaniel says. "All four of us. Ewing went first, then Wayman and Benoit, and then I was just sitting there hoping that my name would be called. I didn't want to be sitting there by myself, waiting for a team to pick me. And when they called my name, I just thanked God that I was able to do something for my family. Anyone who knows me knows that I would come to the gym with jeans and sneakers on. I would have played the game for free. But to be able to take care of my family and still do something that I love...that's what made it so special."

McDaniel was an instant success. He averaged 17.1 points and 8.0 rebounds as a starter during his rookie season. He was also named first-team All-Rookie and *Basketball Digest* co-Rookie of the Year (along with Malone).

"Patrick won the NBA Rookie of the Year award," he says, smiling. Casual acquaintances on draft day, Ewing and McDaniel have formed a close friendship through the years. The two men are now like brothers, and rib each other good-naturedly. "I tell him all the time that he should give me my damn trophy back [laughs]. Patrick will say, 'Man, but I put up numbers,' and I say, 'But you got hurt and only did it for 50 games. I did it for 82 games!' We joke a lot about that. I tell him I'm going to come over to his house and steal my trophy from him."

McDaniel, with his head shaved clean and that intimidating, trademark scowl on display during games, could hardly help contain the joy he felt when away from the court. And who could blame him? The man who grew up idolizing Dr. J was suddenly competing against him. The man who imagined himself as Wes Unseld, or Bobby "Greyhound" Dandridge, or Elvin Hayes was wearing an NBA uniform and playing at some of the same venues.

"I took a little bit of something from all of those guys," gushes McDaniel proudly. "Bobby Dandridge and the Big E—Elvin Hayes—had the turnaround jump shot, and that's the shot that I had to have. I told myself that I was going to master that shot. Dandridge used to shoot it for the Washington Bullets and Milwaukee Bucks. The Big E used to get down on those blocks and shoot it. Unstoppable. Wes Unseld and Moses Malone were all about the rebounding. Those were my guys. People don't give the outlet pass a lot of recognition, but Wes Unseld was the best ever at doing that. If you go back and look at the history of college basketball, he was right there at the top, and I was probably second. I could throw the two-hand outlet, I could throw the one-hand baseball pass—and I could throw both of them on the money. So these are some of the things that I tried to learn from the guys I watched and admired."

The Sonics improved during McDaniel's second season in the league, shocking the heavily favored Dallas Mavericks in the first round of the playoffs. He turned in a 29-point gem in the deciding game. The once-downtrodden Sonics were now building on the foundation of McDaniel, sharpshooter Dale Ellis, and the versatile Tom Chambers. All three players would average more than 20 points per game during the 1986-'87 season, a feat that they would duplicate a year later. Gradually, however, the rebuilding momentum stalled. Chambers was eventually moved, and Shawn Kemp was drafted in the first round of the 1989 NBA Draft.

McDaniel played 15 games for the Sonics during the 1990-'91 season, before being traded to Phoenix. The X-Man was less than a perfect fit for a Suns team that boasted Kevin Johnson, Chambers, Jeff Hornacek, and Dan Majerle, and the following season found himself paired with good pal Ewing in New York. With a formidable frontline of Ewing, McDaniel, and Charles Oakley, the Pat Riley-coached Knicks won 51 games before meeting Michael Jordan and the Chicago Bulls in the

Eastern Conference Semifinals. The intense series went the distance, with Jordan & Co. prevailing in the seventh game.

"There ain't very many games that I said I couldn't get up and walk away from, but I was so sore after that one. It was so physical. It was a brutal war out there—the whole series was like that—but I felt like we should have won that series. We lost Game 1 in Chicago but came back and took Game 2. Patrick had an unbelievable game. I just felt like we had championship potential, but we didn't get the job done when it counted. The Bulls won the series, and went on to win it all."

A contract dispute ended McDaniel's stay in New York after one season, and the unrestricted free agent was available to any team interested in his services. The Boston Celtics wasted little time making contact with X. As the talks progressed, he found out firsthand what it was like to negotiate with the legendary Red Auerbach.

McDaniel: "When I came on my visit to Boston, Red laid the numbers out on the table. He said, 'We know you're worth more than this, but this is all we've got.' Then he said, 'Xavier, being a Celtic is more than money. And now that we've put this money on the table, you ain't leaving this room until you give us an answer.' So I asked him to leave the room for a minute, because I needed to make one phone call. I didn't want to call my girlfriend, I didn't want to call my momma. I told [agent] David Falk that I needed to call one person—Patrick Ewing.

"So Patrick answers and I say, 'Man, he's got me cornered. He's got me cornered in this room, and he won't let me out without an answer.' I asked Patrick what to do, and he tells me to do what's right for me. Red comes back in, we talk some more, and after about 15 minutes I sign the contract. Red shakes my hand and says, 'Welcome to the Celtics family. When you become a Celtic, you become a Celtic for life. No matter where you go in this world, the door is always open as long as I'm alive.' That meant a lot to me."

X-Man played three seasons for the Celtics, this at a time when the franchise was going through significant transition and tragedy. Larry Bird retired prior to his arrival, Kevin McHale and Robert Parish were in serious decline, and Reggie Lewis died of a heart attack following the 1992-'93 season.

"Reggie was a very good person," McDaniel says, "the kind of person who was always helping people. Great leader. When Chris Ford took me out of the starting lineup, Reggie stood behind me and told Coach that he needed to get X back in the lineup. I told Chris that I didn't mind coming off the bench, but Reggie and I worked well together. We had a play that we ran—if he went over the top I'd look for him, or if he went underneath he'd fade to the corner. It was all based on what the defense gave us. But we'd run that play, and it was very successful.

"He was a community-minded guy who always got out and did things for those less fortunate than himself. I just sat in bed and cried when I heard that he'd died. It hurt a whole lot. It hurt so much that that's all I could do—just sit in my room and cry. I miss Reggie."

McDaniel finished his three-year contract with the Celtics and found the team moving in another direction. He played two more seasons in the NBA, both with the New Jersey Nets, before retiring 20 games into the 1997-'98 campaign. Splitting time between homes in Seattle and Columbia, he soon grew bored with his sedate lifestyle and began fixing up houses, a passion that exists today.

"I go into neighborhoods where lots haven't been built on, and I try to buy those lots. That's when I come in with a crew. We do the foundation and the framing. I bought 33 pieces of property in Columbia, South Carolina, and I've got six of them sold. I bought the land for $100,000—you can't buy it up north for that—and I've used my own money to back it all. I didn't go get any loans. It keeps me busy; I get up around 5 a.m. on most days, go to the gym and work out, and then head to the job site. I love basketball, but I also love what I'm doing right now."

Where Have You Gone?

BILL SHARMAN

Hall of Famer Times Two

His home office is a mini-museum, with hundreds of rare pictures, trophies, glassed-encased basketballs of historical significance, championship ring displays, jerseys, bats, and plaques lining bookshelves and covering almost every inch of wall space. Near his desk stands a life-sized cardboard photo image of himself as a crewcut young player wearing a No. 11 Southern California basketball uniform.

As Bill Sharman discusses his 54-year career in pro basketball, he uses the words "fortunate" and "lucky" to describe his remarkable success in the game he loves. Truth is "luck" had nothing to do with it. The former Celtics guard, who was elected to the Hall of Fame for his achievements as a player in 1976, is a winner and a champion because of hard work, tremendous talent, intelligence, and, most importantly, an enthusiasm that only grows stronger with each passing year.

"I've been blessed," Sharman says. "I've been a part of 15 pro basketball championship teams—four as a player with the Boston Celtics, three as a coach, two as general manager of the Los Angeles Lakers, three as president of the Lakers, and three as special consultant for the Lakers. However, the one I remember and cherish the most is the Celtics' first championship in 1957 versus the St. Louis Hawks. We won [the seventh game] in double-overtime by two points. My shots weren't falling and

AP/WWP

BILL SHARMAN

College: Southern California '50 | Height: 6'1" | Weight: 175 lbs.
Position: Guard | Years with Celtics: 1951-'52 through 1960-'61

Notes: Traded by the Fort Wayne Pistons with Bob Brannum for the rights to Charlie Share in 1951. His No. 21 jersey was retired on October 15, 1966. Member of four NBA championship teams while with the Celtics. Enshrined in the Naismith Memorial Basketball Hall of Fame as a player and a coach.

Cousy was struggling a little, but we had such a great bunch of guys that everyone just knew we'd find a way to win. ... We had the ultimate confidence in one another.

"My whole experience in Boston was unbelievable. It was such a privilege and thrill to play for the great Red Auerbach. My teammates were the best, and the fans were always so supportive. I couldn't have asked for a better experience."

Regarded as the NBA's premiere pure shooter throughout the 1950s, the six-foot-one Sharman led the league in free-throw percentage seven times, including five in a row. His reliable outside jumpers, usually set up by one of Bob Cousy's on-target, often miraculous passes, were the perfect complement to the Celtics' inside attack, led by Bill Russell's offensive rebounding and Tommy Heinsohn's hook shots and short pull-up jumpers.

"Cousy would kid me about all the shots I got," recalls Sharman, who spent his first five Celtic offseasons as an outfielder in the Brooklyn Dodgers organization. "The funniest moment I had as a Celtic came in the '57 All-Star game at Boston. I grabbed a defensive rebound and spotted Bob all alone upcourt. I threw a full-court baseball pass towards him. He jumped for the ball, but it went over his outstretched hand and into the basket. As Cousy came back down the court, he faked being angry and said, "Just like I always tell people, you never pass the ball to your teammate—even if they're wide open.'"

According to the legendary Auerbach, Sharman was more than merely a student of the game. "He was way ahead of his time," the former Celtics coach says. "On the day of every game, Bill would get up early in the morning and find a gym where he could work on his shot and his conditioning. Eventually I decided that if a great shooter like Sharman believed in it, then a light morning workout might help everyone on the team. That's how 'shootarounds' began. After we began doing it, every team copied us. Then there were also Bill's ideas about nutrition and proper rest. He ate specific meals at specific times. He knew the value of getting a good night's sleep. Every game day he took a nap for an hour. If he didn't get enough rest, he'd be angry with the world."

Sharman, who was selected to the All-NBA team seven times, helped the Celtics win four titles before retiring at age 35. "The guy probably could have played another three or four years, but I knew Bill was itching to coach," said Auerbach. "Whenever he was on the bench, he'd ask me a million questions about strategy, about substitutions. Almost every time he'd make a suggestion, it would be a good one. And I was smart enough to realize he had an incredible mind for the game."

That knowledge paid off handsomely for Sharman and the teams he coached. In his first year on the bench, Sharman's Cleveland Pipers won the ABL title. In 1971 he led the Utah Stars to an ABA championship. When he took over as coach of the Lakers in 1971, critics said his players were too old and too stubborn to be very "coachable." In particular, the media contended that Lakers star Wilt Chamberlain, at 35, would likely prove to be a major headache. At a casual preseason one-on-one meeting, Sharman managed to convince his seven foot-one center that fastbreak basketball—and morning shootarounds—would be the keys to success.

"If this team was going to win, I knew that Wilt and I had to get off to a good start. Everything went well until I mentioned that I was going to have mandatory game-day morning shootarounds," Sharman recalls. "I expected Wilt, who had a reputation for being a night owl, might be upset at having to get up so often early in the morning. But, to my surprise, he didn't put up a stink. Instead Wilt told me, 'I'll go along with the idea, and we'll try it. If I think it will help the team, I'll do it.' Getting Wilt on my side from the beginning meant more than I can explain. He just had to buy into my beliefs, or the team would be in trouble."

L.A. proceeded to win 69 games that season as Chamberlain, bloodshot eyes and all, went through morning shootarounds without complaint. Scoring more than 120 points a game for the season, Sharman's Lakers easily won the NBA title.

In all, the former Celtic guard coached 11 seasons before he was forced to leave the sidelines for good due to a mysterious vocal chord ailment that left his voice at a hoarse whisper. Six times he took his team to league finals, three times winning a championship. Along the way, he was voted Coach of the Year in the ABL (1962), Coach of the Year in the ABA (1970), and NBA Coach of the Year (1972).

"Not only was the man a tireless worker, he was an innovator. Bill was the first coach to study film on a daily basis," said former Celtics teammate K.C. Jones, who was hired by Sharman in 1971 to be the first assistant coach in Lakers history. "He did everything possible to make sure his team would be prepared, both mentally and physically. Because he regularly put in 18-hour workdays, his players believed and respected him. I mean totally.

"As a former player, Bill realized the importance of making sure everyone had a little fun at practices. For example, he might tell Wilt to play the point guard position in a scrimmage. Then everyone would break up laughing as Chamberlain dribbled upcourt and launched the funniest looking 25-foot jumpers you'd ever see. He found ways of livening things up rather than having the same old routine."

After leaving the coaching ranks, Sharman became L.A.'s general manager. Directing the Lakers' personnel moves, he was instrumental is molding the '80 and '82 title teams. Choosing to leave the GM post in 1983 due to continuing vocal problems, Sharman became a special consultant to the Lakers, a position he still holds today. It is far from an honorary title. He regularly attends Lakers home games and then writes evaluation reports for both the front office and the coaching staff. When the team is on the road, he spends time scouting college talent on TV and with videotape.

Inducted to the Hall of Fame as a player in 1976, Sharman was re-enshrined last year for his achievements as a coach. He joined John Wooden and Lenny Wilkens as the only men to be honored twice by the institution. Still an active golfer with a handicap of "ugh," as he puts it, Bill and his wife, Joyce, reside in Playa del Ray, California. They have four children and six grandchildren.

Where Have You Gone?

HANK FINKEL

"High Henry"

He was the man who replaced the retired Bill Russell in the Celtics' starting lineup. Of course, it was the ultimate "can't-win" situation. Hank Finkel, despite an abundance of desire and hustle, just didn't possess one-tenth of Russell's quickness and skills, as well as his instinctive knack for playing the game. And the Boston Garden fans were not at all pleased when massive muscular giants such as Wilt Chamberlain, Willis Reed, Walt Bellamy, and Wes Unseld bullied their way to the basket as Boston's seven-foot center attempted to simply hold his defensive position in the paint and limit his opponents' production.

Rookie Celtics head coach Tom Heinsohn experimented with different frontcourt lineups, using Finkel at both center and power forward, usually as a starter, although he also was occasionally brought in as the sixth man. But without Russell and Sam Jones, who had also retired, the 1969-'70 Celtics struggled throughout the season and finished out of the playoffs for the first time since 1950, with a record of 34-48.

Finkel was Public Enemy No. 1, as the fans showered him with choruses of boos, mixed with occasional derogatory comments. No one was more upset with the crowd's behavior than Coach Heinsohn.

"No reporter has ever heard one word out of my mouth about Henry Finkel's effort," Heinsohn said after one loss in which Finkel was the

146

AP/WWF

HANK FINKEL

College: Dayton '66 | **Height:** 7'0" | **Weight:** 245 lbs.
Position: Center | **Years with Celtics:** 1969-'70 through 1974-'75

Notes: Sold by the San Diego Clippers to the Boston Celtics for cash
and a draft choice on August 22, 1969. Member of one NBA championship
team with the Boston Celtics (1974).

constant target of crowd critics. "Hank's come in here and has been a total professional. I think our fans should be supportive, not negative. Henry Finkel is not the reason we're losing. It's not fair for him to be singled out as the symbol for this team's problems. You lose a Bill Russell, and there are going to be consequences. We'll get better; it just won't happen overnight."

Finkel, who led the nation in field goal percentage as a senior at the University of Dayton, was drafted in the fourth round of the 1966 draft by the Lakers and played 27 games as a rookie, with such greats as Elgin Baylor, Jerry West, and Gail Goodrich as teammates. Selected in the 1967 expansion draft, Finkel then spent two seasons with the San Diego Rockets before being traded to Boston.

"People said I was acquired to be Russell's replacement," says Finkel, who split the staring center responsibilities with 6'9" Rich Johnson. "That bothered me, because everyone knew no one in the NBA could 'replace' Bill Russell. Heck, I was just an average reserve player. Before I even put on the Celtics uniform, I knew I wasn't a legitimate starting center in this league. I didn't kid myself. I didn't have great talent, so I just made up my mind to try and outwork whoever was matched up against me. But the Boston fans, at least during my first year as a Celtic, had some high expectations about my abilities. I knew I wasn't capable of playing at the level they thought I could."

The season took its toll on Finkel, who never complained about the unfair treatment he had received at the Garden. "I have to admit I thought about retiring," he says. "It wasn't an easy year. I'd come home after a game and just feel totally drained and depressed. The money I was making wasn't that great, so I thought I might move to San Diego, where I had some good business contacts from when I played there. Fortunately, Red Auerbach, Tommy, and a few of my close teammates talked me out of it."

To his credit, Finkel gradually won over fans with his humble, friendly personality. The fact that he was always willing to sign autographs and take the time to talk with fans enabled him to go from goat to fan favorite in a year's time.

"At seven feet, I was hard to miss," he says. "Thanks to Johnny Most, who gave me the nickname 'High Henry,' people would come up to me and just want to say hello and tell me they were rooting for me. It was flattering, and I enjoyed just talking basketball with the fans because they cared so much about the Celtics."

Boston drafted Dave Cowens and obtained power forward Paul Silas, a rebounding machine, in the offseason following Finkel's first year as a Celtic.

"Tommy used me to back up Dave and even Paul at times," recalls Finkel. "The key thing is that I was almost always playing next to an All-Star who could score and rebound. I'd block out on the boards, set picks, and occasionally roll to the basket for an easy layup. Basketball was fun again."

Retirement left Finkel's mind, and he thoroughly enjoyed his new role as a reserve.

"I like to think I was a team player who knew the game. I knew I wasn't going to outjump too many guys, so I would try to always get good rebounding position and then box guys out," the gangly, wide-shouldered Finkel says. "On offense, I'd take the open shot because I had a fair jumper, but the thing I did best was set picks for our scorers, especially for John Havlicek. John and I worked well together. I remember one game in Buffalo where I was standing in the frontcourt and John had just gotten a defensive rebound. [Braves guard] Randy Smith, one of the fastest players in the league, started chasing John. Havlicek saw me sticking out my butt to set a pick and took off towards me at full speed. Well, Randy Smith never saw what was coming, and he just crumbled when he ran into me. That left John with an easy jumper for an uncontested basket.

"In the NBA, if you can set a pick that frees guys like Havlicek, [Don] Nelson, [Paul] Westphal or [JoJo] White for just a quarter of a second, they will come off the screen and hit 70 percent of those shots. My job was to give them that split second to free them up for a jumper. I took pride in doing all the little things for the team which made the job of our All-Star players a little easier."

Following the 1974-'75 season, his sixth year as a Celtic, "High Henry" decided to retire. "Of course winning the '74 championship was the highlight of my career," he says. "Truthfully, though, the greatest thrill of my years with Boston was just enjoying the tremendous camaraderie. I made so many great friends. The guys I played with, from the starters to the reserves, were all so unselfish, so special. I don't think any team was as close as we were."

Finkel planned on moving his family to San Diego until Jerry Volk, Jan Volk's father, called with a job offer. Jerry Volk was opening a new business and thought the popular Finkel, with his easy-going, straightforward personality would make an excellent salesman.

"Things were going well for me financially and personally," says Finkel. "Then, one night at a Celtics game I was told that Jerry had passed away suddenly. The man had always treated me so well. I knew things wouldn't be the same without him as my boss, so I eventually quit.

"My degree from Dayton was in education, so I thought about becoming a teacher. Revere High School offered me the varsity basketball coaching job, but they didn't have a teaching opening. Then I received an offer to coach at Robert Morris University, just outside Pittsburgh. By then, my family just loved living in the Boston area so much, I couldn't bring myself to relocate. My old teammate, Don Nelson, who was coaching the Bucks, offered me a chance to scout part-time for him, but I really wanted a job that would allow me to spend time at home. In the end, I opened up my own office furniture sales company. I've stayed with it for almost 29 years now, and it's been very rewarding."

Finkel resides in Lynnfield with his wife, Kathleen. The couple has two children, Dennis and Wenda, and three grandchildren. "Even today, I'll be in a local store or just walking down the street and someone will yell out, 'Hey, High Henry, how ya doing?' I never get tired of it. I'm 63 now, so it's a nice feeling to be remembered after all these years."

ERNIE BARRETT

The Gift

His basketball career began in a Kansas railroad town, and while his legacy will forever be defined by his contributions to Kansas State University—first as an All-America guard with a feathery touch from outside, and then as the school's athletic director and fund-raiser extraordinaire—Ernie Barrett will also remain deeply woven into the fabric of professional basketball's greatest franchise. Selected in the first round of the 1951 NBA draft by Red Auerbach and the Boston Celtics, Barrett's most important contribution may have come years later, as Auerbach wrestled over whom to select with the fourth overall pick in 1970. The choices were New Mexico State big man Sam Lacey, or Florida State's undersized-but-energetic Dave Cowens. Auerbach respected Barrett's opinion immensely. He also knew that Barrett, then the K-State athletic director, had seen Lacey in action against the Wildcats. Barrett came away from that contest less than enamored with the Aggies' 6'10" center, and he shared his evaluation with Auerbach on the eve of the draft. The Celtics patriarch heeded Barrett's advice and selected Cowens at No. 4; and while Lacey would go on to play 13 solid-yet-unspectacular seasons primarily with the New York Knicks, Cowens would win two NBA championships with Boston and wind up in the Naismith Memorial Basketball Hall of Fame.

ERNIE BARRETT

**College: Kansas State '51 | Height: 6'3" | Weight: 180 lbs.
Position: Guard | Years with Celtics: 1953-'54 and 1955-'56**

Notes: First-round draft choice of the Boston Celtics in 1951. Played two seasons
for the Celtics. Credited with convincing Red Auerbach to draft Dave Cowens.

Today, Barrett is the director of development for the Intercollegiate
Athletic Agency of his alma mater, where he oversees the school's fund-
raising efforts. Under his watch, Barrett has been instrumental in raising
money for major improvements to the K-State sports facilities. He credits
his education in public relations for helping him become a better
communicator in his current position.

"The ability to communicate effectively is important in fund raising,"
he says emphatically. "It helps open doors and checkbooks, both of which
are very important in what I do."

Barrett may have grown up in the shadow of the Great Depression,
but the hard times did little to dampen his can-do spirit or quell his
outsized personality, gifts that have served him well throughout an
illustrious career capped by a statue in his honor and the unofficial title of
"Mr. K-State." His palm-crushing handshake has become both his calling
card and the stuff of legend. Years earlier, however, his calling card was his
dead-eye shooting, a gift that helped propel a tiny Kansas high school to
its only state basketball championship and earned Barrett a scholarship to
Kansas State University.

"We won the state championship in 1947," Barrett says, "which is
still the last time a team from Wellington has won a state title in
basketball. That '47 Wellington squad had plenty of talent, fine players
like Harold Rogers who went on to play for coach [Henry] Iba at
Oklahoma State University. Our coach was John Floyd, and I credit him
with all of my success as a basketball player. He was the person who taught
me the fundamentals, and the one who really helped me to improve my

shooting. I was a six-foot-one center in high school—that should tell you about the height we had on that team—and I went on to play guard at Kansas State. I probably wouldn't have made it as a college player if Coach Floyd hadn't worked with me on my outside shooting. Even back then you just didn't find many 6'1" centers playing major college basketball. K-State had a 6'5" guard that first year I was on the team, and the Boston Celtics had players like Bob Donham who were bigger than me. So learning to play away from the basket was a tremendous help, and Coach Floyd was the person who had the most to do with that development."

Barrett joined the Wildcats in 1947, the same season legendary coach Jack Gardner—who would later earn the distinction as the only coach to take two schools to the Final Four twice—returned to the helm at K-State. The union proved just the tonic for the once-moribund basketball program, as the Wildcats improved their win total by 10 games and posted a winning season for the first time in 16 years. By 1951 the circle was complete; K-State toppled mighty Oklahoma State before battling Adolph Rupp's Kentucky Wildcats in the Final Four title game. UK may have won that game, shutting down K-State with rock-hard defense in the second half, but Barrett capped his dream season in style. The talented senior received All-America honors and quickly found himself the draft-day property of the Boston Celtics.

"Unfortunately I injured my shoulder against Oklahoma State in the West Regional Final in Kansas City—there were only two Regionals then—and wasn't able to play to my fullest against Kentucky. We beat BYU 64-54 in the semifinals and then defeated Oklahoma State to advance to the championship game. It was the worst defeat Coach Iba had ever suffered at Oklahoma State. I took a charge in that game and ended up with a deep muscle bruise. We were going to shoot it up with Novocain but Coach Gardner was against it. He thought it might be injurious to my health, and he didn't want to cause any long-term damage to the shoulder.

"Kentucky was coached by Rupp, and they had some really great players on that team. They had Bill Spivey, who scored 22 points in that game, and a couple of other pretty good players in Cliff Hagan and Frank Ramsey. We jumped out to an early lead and were up by two at the half,

29-27, but couldn't hold them off after intermission. Kentucky dominated the boards and won the game by ten."

Barrett joined a Celtics team boasting a fiery, young coach named Red Auerbach, but the arrival of the great Bill Russell remained several years way. The NBA was still in its infancy. Fans flocked to the college game, while the NBA struggled to attract a mainstream audience and earn a place alongside baseball and football as one of the country's major professional sports. Players such as Barrett were vital in this regard; they possessed valuable name recognition, a key component in selling the league to a reluctant public. Barrett, however, did not immediately join the Celtics.

"I had a two-year military obligation," he explains, "so my 'rookie' year [1953-'54] was actually two years [after I was drafted]. Red started me every game during the exhibition season, opposite Bob Cousy, for what amounted to 15-20 games over a three-week period. We basically barnstormed all over New England."

But then things changed dramatically for Barrett once the regular season began. "I didn't get into a single game during the first 35 games, at which point [Celtic owner] Walter Brown went to Red and wanted to know why I wasn't playing. [Brown] looked at me as the team's first-round selection in 1951 and figured I should be seeing some action. Needless to say, I was on Walter Brown's side," Barrett recalls with a chuckle. "So I ended up playing more during the second half of the season, sharing time with the great Bill Sharman."

Despite the lack of playing time, Barrett and Auerbach developed a strong relationship that lasts to this day.

"Coach Auerbach amazed me with the way he handled the players," says Barrett, "and with how he was able to keep them all happy and ready to play. He knew which players responded well to the screaming, and he knew which ones to motivate in a more subtle way. There really is no comparison between Red and anyone else. He was extremely intelligent, a real genius."

As for Auerbach, he clearly respects and values Barrett's opinion. Drafting Cowens is a prime example.

"That's exactly how it happened," Barrett replies, when asked about the dynamics behind Boston's first-round selection in the 1970 NBA Draft. "I saw Sam Lacey, so I knew what he was capable of. Not to say that he couldn't play, but I just thought Cowens had much better mobility and could shoot the ball better. Red was leaning toward choosing Lacey, and he called to ask who I thought was the better player. To me, Cowens was a perfect fit in the Celtics' system. He could get up and down the court, and he could run all day long. And he was intense. Red took my advice, and it worked out well for everyone involved."

Unlikely to take a starting job from either Cousy or Sharman, Barrett returned to Kansas following his first season determined to begin a career in coaching. The stay would be short-lived, as the NBA adopted the 24-second shot clock following the 1954-'55 season. Auerbach, sensing that the change would be a boon to free-wheeling, dead-eye players like Barrett, wasted little time in placing a call to coax the All-American out of retirement. Barrett gladly accepted, playing one more successful season in a Celtics uniform before returning to his beloved K-State for good. (The 1955-'56 Boston Celtics averaged a league-high 106 points per game, with super-sub Barrett averaging 20.2 minutes per game off the bench.)

"I wanted to play—I'm a competitor," says Barrett. "Red thought that this change suited my style of play, so he asked me to come back. I said that I would, but only if I got a chance to play. Red was true to his word—I played in every game that season. I really wanted to stay on, but the next season the Celtics got Heinsohn and Russell. Tex Winter was the head coach at K-State at the time, and he offered me a position as assistant coach. I jumped at the opportunity, and I went to work at my alma mater. I've been there ever since."

Barrett's name is indelibly linked to Kansas State University, his legend there secure. He has been inducted into the K-State Athletic Hall of Fame, both as a player and as an administrator. He has been part and parcel of the university for six decades, first as an All-America basketball player, later as the athletics director, and now as a gifted fund-raiser.

Still he remains closely connected to the Boston Celtics. He counts Bob Cousy among his closest friends, and his relationship with Auerbach is especially noteworthy. Barrett played alongside Celtic tough man Bob Brannum in his first stint with the team, and then played with "Jungle" Jim Loscutoff two years later. And then there is Dave Cowens. Had Auerbach selected Lacey, those championships in 1974 and 1976—banners 12 and 13 on your scorecard—probably wouldn't have happened at all. Barrett's advice validated Auerbach's faith in his one-time sharpshooter, and proved to be the perfect gift indeed.

WAYNE EMBRY

Central Character

Johnny Most nicknamed him "The Wall," a tribute to the bone-rattling picks that he set as a member of the Boston Celtics, and today his considerable influence stretches from the NBA to Wall Street and back again. Wayne Embry's latest foray into professional basketball is with the Toronto Raptors, where he serves as senior basketball advisor to the president. Embry joined the Raptors organization in June 2004 as senior advisor to the general manager.

"You always face issues when you are trying to build a team," Embry says flatly. Unafraid of a challenge, the hall of famer is rolling up his sleeves yet again to do just that. In his new role, Embry will report directly to Richard Peddie, president and chief executive officer of Maple Leaf Sports & Entertainment, as his advisor on all matters directly related to the Raptors. "It is no different here. We have got to address a number of issues as we try to make this franchise a success. Things aren't all well there yet, but I feel that my track record as an executive speaks for itself. I just hope that I can play an integral part in this team's transformation. I hate to lose. I have a passion for winning, so hopefully I can have some input and make some contribution into that happening."

The man knows his hoops, no question about that. But spend a few minutes talking to Wayne Embry, and it isn't long before you realize that

WAYNE EMBRY

**College: Miami (Ohio) '58 | Height: 6'8" | Weight: 255 lbs.
Position: Center | Years with Celtics: 1966-'67 through 1967-'68**

Notes: Won an NBA championship with Boston in 1968. Inducted into the
Naismith Memorial Basketball Hall of Fame as a contributor on October 1, 1999.

this former NBA All-Star is far more than a link to the days when legends
such as Russell and Chamberlain ruled the basketball universe. Embry is
as relevant now as he was then, only in areas that extend far beyond the
hardwood. Backboards have morphed into boardrooms. Bone-crunching
picks have given way to civic stewardship. From trading elbows with Willis
Reed to rubbing elbows with Alan Greenspan, Embry is the rare athlete
who has eclipsed his own star power in terms of off-the-court
accomplishments.

Alan Greenspan?

"I'm a member of the board for the Bank of Cleveland," Embry
replies when pressed for more. "The Bank of Cleveland reports to the
Central Bank, and we play a large role in shaping monetary and economic
policy. It's interesting work and very rewarding."

Clearly, Embry's management skills have served him well as an NBA
executive, business owner, and board member. He is currently winding
down a five-year term with the Federal Reserve Bank, making decisions
that impact the economy on a global scale. He has his new gig with the
Raptors. And he has been a pioneer in terms of breaking the NBA front-
office color barrier—Embry became the NBA's first African American
general manager in 1972, and in 1994 was named the first African
American NBA team president and chief operating officer.

"I was the GM in Milwaukee for eight seasons," he says. "I began
working in the front office in 1971. The owners knew that I had a close
relationship with Oscar Robertson, so they asked me to make a call on
their behalf. I made the key inquiry for them. Having Kareem [then Lew

Alcindor] and Oscar on the same team was an unbelievable combination for us. We won the championship that year, and the next season I was promoted to general manager."

Embry's relationship with Robertson dated back to their playing days in Cincinnati. The two men remain close and speak often by telephone.

"Oscar Robertson, in my opinion, is the best to ever play the game of basketball. We were roommates when I was with the Royals, and it was an honor to be on the same team with him. He certainly enhanced my career. He had a great impact on me, but his influence extended beyond basketball and into the bigger picture of life. As you can tell, I have a tremendous amount of respect and admiration for Oscar Robertson."

Born and raised in Ohio, Embry began his basketball career at Tecumseh High School before starring at Miami of Ohio, where he was a two-time honorable mention All-America selection, and where his number has long since been retired. Back then, Embry stayed in school the entire four years; in his new role with the Raptors, he sees an entirely different landscape.

Embry: "Well, today you see guys go from high school directly to the pros, which is something that just didn't happen when I played. You have to factor that into the decision-making process. Even if that had been the trend during my era, I simply wasn't prepared to play professional basketball. College was the best route for me. I was a somewhat of a slow developer—as a freshman I wasn't even the best player on the team—but by my sophomore season I'd improved in every aspect of my game and had much greater confidence in my ability. I blossomed during my junior year, and things really took off from that point on."

As a pro, Embry was a five-time All-Star for the Cincinnati Royals, playing alongside such legendary stars as the Big O (Robertson) and Jerry Lucas. An NBA championship proved elusive, however, as the Royals routinely failed to supplant the Boston Celtics as kings of the East. In a classic case of 'If you can't beat 'em, join 'em', Red Auerbach acquired Embry in 1966 as a backup to the incomparable Bill Russell. After being dethroned by Chamberlain and the Philadelphia 76ers in 1967, the

Celtics—with Embry—were back on top, winning a league-best tenth NBA championship.

"There was a great sense of relief," he says. "After playing the game for so long, and after being frustrated by Russell and the Celtics all of those years, it was just a great relief to finally be able to win a championship."

Embry's natural proclivity toward management left him in awe of legendary coach Red Auerbach. Often referred to as a genius, Auerbach's approach to the game—especially the way he handled players of all stature and accomplishment—intrigued the aspiring front office executive.

"Red had a tremendous management style," says Embry. "It was at the foundation of his success as a coach and general manager. You look at the way he motivated players, and you begin to understand the man's talent. He instinctively knew that some guys would respond to screaming, while others responded better to criticism behind closed doors. So the way he managed a Tom Heinsohn was completely different from the way he managed a Bob Cousy or a Bill Russell. There is a lot to say for that. I adopted and emulated that style in both sports and business, and it has worked well for me."

And then there is Russell. Did Embry learn anything from the man who won on every level imaginable?

"Russell was the greatest competitor and the greatest winner in the history of professional sports. The Celtics won 11 championships during his 13 years with the team, which, in my mind, ranks as the greatest dynasty ever. The New York Yankees may have won more championships, but those are spread out over decades. To win 11 in 13 is an incredible accomplishment.

"I learned a lot from being around Russell and immersing myself in the championship culture that he was responsible for developing there. He was once asked about winning and said, 'If you have to play, you might as well win.' When you think about things in those terms, then you can't help but expect more out of yourself. As an executive practicing management skills, those are valuable words to live by."

In 1985, Embry's management skills would be put to the ultimate test. The moribund Cleveland Cavaliers, mired in a losing funk that threatened the very existence of the franchise, hired Embry to reverse the fortunes of the basketball faithful in Northern Ohio. Under his direction as vice-president and general manager, the Cavaliers won 40 or more games 10 times, 50 or more on three occasions, and advanced to the Eastern Conference Finals in 1992.

"Turning the Cavaliers into a winner was an awesome challenge," he says, "but it was well worth it. Like I said, winning is very important to me. To help the franchise overcome years of underachieving and mismanagement is something of which I can be proud."

Embry was promoted to executive vice-president position with the club in 1992. Two seasons later he broke the NBA's color barrier once again, becoming the first African American NBA team president and chief operating officer. Recognition for his work with the Cavs was never far away: Embry earned *The Sporting News* Executive of the Year honor in 1992 and 1998, as well as the *Sports Illustrated* Executive of the Year award in 1998.

"It's nice to be recognized," says Embry. "But more than that, it's also very rewarding to see all of your hard work pay off. When you look at where the Cleveland franchise was when I took over, and where it was when I left, that's really the most important thing. The Cavaliers were a much more viable product at the end of my stay."

The ultimate recognition came on October 1, 1999, when Embry was inducted into the Naismith Memorial Basketball Hall of Fame—not as a player, despite the All-America honors, All-Star appearances, and world championship ring, but as a contributor known for his shrewd moves and winning management style.

"Being honored in that way was something I never dreamed of, and it makes you realize that not many people get that kind of recognition. My goal was simply to do a good job. Obviously, I'm very honored to be included in such an elite group who has already been enshrined into the Hall of Fame. I'm pleased and I feel privileged to be part of that group. It was definitely the highlight of my career."

Now the man know as "The Wall" is putting the accolades in the rearview mirror and embracing yet another heady challenge. And if history is any indication, the Toronto Raptors will be much better off because of it. Among Embry's responsibilities will be educating the board of directors on basketball-related matters.

"I'm there to talk to them about basketball," Embry says. "I have gained over 46 years of experience and expertise, and I'm looking forward to just helping in a small way and a big way. I'm very impressed with the fans and their enthusiasm. And they should be rewarded with a winning basketball team."

JOE FORTE

Starting from Scratch

Mention Joe Forte's name to any knowledgeable Celtics fan, and you're liable to evoke a response that includes a string of derogatory adjectives. Although his stay in Boston lasted only a single season, the six-foot-four guard became the symbol of all that went wrong for the team during the Rick Pitino Era.

After opting for the NBA after a spectacular sophomore season at the University of North Carolina in which he averaged 21 points, six rebounds, and nearly four assists per game, Forte was selected by Boston with the 21st pick of the 2001 draft. The Celtics, in particular Red Auerbach, were so enamored with his potential that they passed up a chance to take either Tony Parker or Jamaal Tinsley, both point guards, in order to take the former DeMatha High McDonald's All-American.

"I guess my problems began the first time I was told that [the Celtics] planned to use me as a point guard," Forte says. "Right away, I wasn't happy because I had always been a shooter, a scorer. At UNC, people always compared me to [Michael] Jordan, at least in the way that I always wanted the ball when the game was on the line. Now the Celtics were saying that basically if I was going to play, it would have to be at the point. I didn't agree. But I figured I could prove to them I could play any position and still score."

APWWP

JOE FORTE

**College: North Carolina '03 | Height: 6'4" | Weight: 194 lbs.
Position: Guard | Years with Celtics: 2001-'02**

Notes: Selected in the first round of the 2001 NBA draft by Boston. Appeared in eight games during his rookie season. Traded with Kenny Anderson and Vitaly Potapenko to the Seattle SuperSonics for Vin Baker and Shammond Williams on July 22, 2002.

Truth is Forte was a classic "tweener," too small to guard an NBA-caliber shooting guard and too inexperienced to be a true playmaker. Coming out of UNC, his ballhandling skills were not close to being at an NBA point guard's level. Plus, Forte had a "shoot first, pass second" approach to the game. As Mavericks scout Kevin Stacom, an ex-Celtic, often says, "There's no such thing as a converted two guard. If a player has a shooter's mentality, he's never going to be able to change into a point."

Forte wasted no time making a conscious decision to rebel. Over the course of his rookie year, he showed up late for three consecutive practices, sat in the locker room during games instead of being on the bench, and even taunted Celtic teammates and the coaching staff by wearing a Magic Johnson Lakers jersey to a pregame meeting.

"I was angry at not playing, and I was immature," he says now. "I was only 20 years old and I couldn't handle it. I did all the wrong things. I know that now. I wanted to play and prove myself, but that wasn't happening. Every time I did something wrong, I thought I was proving a point, letting [the coaches] know I wasn't happy with my situation. In reality, I was burying myself deeper."

Forte would play a total of 39 minutes during his tantrum-filled rookie year. Shortly after the season ended, the Celtics, considering themselves fortunate, were able to dump the malcontent, who was guaranteed for two more years, in a package deal with Seattle that sent Forte, along with Kenny Anderson and Vitaly Potapenko, to the Sonics in exchange for Vin Baker and Shammond Williams.

The change in scenery did nothing to nothing to improve Forte's brat-like behavior. "I was still being used strictly as a point guard, behind Gary Payton and Kenny Anderson," Forte says. "Right away, I knew I wasn't going to get any minutes. I was frustrated and depressed. I separated myself from everybody else on the team."

Instead of viewing his new situation as an opportunity to redeem himself for his well-publicized disruptive conduct in Boston, Forte chose to continue being a pest. On March 26, 2003, he self-destructed once again. Before a game in Seattle against Washington, he boldly walked into the Sonics locker room wearing a Michael Jordan Wizards jersey, as his teammates scowled at him with contempt. Following the game, a six-point Seattle defeat, Forte went into the shower room and began to loudly sing, purposefully to annoy his teammates. His obnoxious conduct was too much of a personal insult for Sonics center Jerome James to ignore. He attacked Forte and had to be restrained by teammates. As a result of the incident, Forte was suspended for a game and fined $11,000; James was not punished at all. Seattle management had made its point. It was clear Forte's Sonic career was nearing an end.

One week after his second dismal pro season concluded, Forte was driving from New York to his home in Washington, D.C., when he was stopped for speeding. When the police searched his car, they found marijuana and a .22-caliber gun. "I wasn't mad, I just didn't care about anything, including being arrested," he says. "I felt like nobody else cared about me, why should I [care about myself]?"

As expected, the Sonics waived Forte just before their 2003 camp opened. And as expected, no other NBA club had any interest in signing him. "Honestly, yes, I thought someone would give me a chance. When that didn't happen, I went home and just hung out by myself," Forte says. "In high school and in college, someone was always right there to show me the right things to do. Once I got to the NBA, I was on my own. And I didn't know how to act. No one was there to say, 'You're screwing things up for yourself.'"

After a year of self-imposed exile, Forte opted to play in the NBDL, the NBA's development league. "When I was cut by the Sonics, I told everyone that I'd never play in that league," he says. "It was like, 'I played at UNC and I was an NBA first-round draft choice. I am not going to ride buses from city to city, eat meals at McDonald's, and play at that level.' I just wasn't going to do it."

But after talking with his first college coach, Bill Guthridge, Forte changed his mind. "[Guthridge] made me understand that when I was in the NBA, I couldn't handle not being a star. He said that I messed up because I couldn't handle being an end-of-the-bench sub in that league. He told me that now I had to prove something. I had to show that I had grown up, that I could handle the pressure, and that I could be in control of things even if things weren't going the way I wished."

Guthridge made one more point. He bluntly warned Forte that he might never make it back to the NBA. "The important thing for him to regain is his reputation," the former UNC head coach said when Forte joined the NBDL. "I'm concerned about Joe Forte, the person. I want to see him succeed in life. If he makes a comeback in basketball, that's a bonus. I hope he views things in that same light."

It appears Forte has indeed undergone an attitude adjustment. As a member of the NBDL-champion Altitude of Ashville, North Carolina, Forte was steady, although not spectacular throughout the 2004-'05 season. Playing both guard positions, he averaged 11.9 points on 48-percent shooting. As the team's sixth man, he provided a modest 2.3 assists a game.

According to Altitude head coach Joey Meyer, he clearly made positive strides. "Basically, he'd come off the bench and give us an immediate scoring lift," he said. "As for playing the point, he's still learning with each game. Personally I think of Joe as just a guard—without any labels. He definitely has skills and potential."

Whether any NBA team will give him a legitimate opportunity, though, remains questionable. "I can't predict what the future holds for Joe," says NBDL official Chris Alberts. "What I can definitely say is that he did a good job on the court and in the community. He represented his team and the NBDL well."

By Bill Guthridge's standards, that means that Forte had a dream season.

Where Have You Gone?

MARVIN BARNES

No More Slips

Throughout the decade of the 1970s, Marvin Barnes was given numerous opportunities to fulfill both his potential as a basketball player and as a person. Perhaps the greatest of these chances came when he was traded to the Celtics following the 1977-'78 season as part of the franchise swap between Boston and the San Diego Clippers.

By then, the former Providence College star had already justly earned a reputation as a supremely talented, team-oriented player whose erratic off-the-court behavior created constant turmoil. In fact, he was well on the way toward self-destruction.

Drafted by the 76ers with the second overall pick of the 1974 draft behind only Portland's choice of Bill Walton, Barnes opted to forgo signing with Philadelphia and instead sign a $2 million contract with the ABA's St. Louis Spirits. As the league's rookie of the year, the muscular 6'9" forward averaged 24 points and 15.7 rebounds per game. Still, the warning signs for trouble were all there.

"I was young, I was wild, and I had a ton of money," Barnes recalls. "I'd be late for a lot of practices. I'd miss team flights and charter my own plane to wherever we were playing. I did what I pleased. Because of the numbers I put up, management never really got too upset. My attitude was, 'If they don't care what I do, I don't care [what I do].'"

MARVIN BARNES

**College: Providence '74 | Height: 6'9" | Weight: 220 lbs.
Position: Forward | Years with Celtics: 1978-'79**

Notes: The Providence All-American and ABA Rookie of the Year was traded by the San Diego Clippers with Nate Archibald, Billy Knight, and future draft choices to Boston for Kermit Washington, Kevin Kunnert, Sidney Wicks, and the rights to Freeman Williams on August 4, 1978. Waived on February 7, 1979.

M.L. Carr, who played alongside Barnes in St. Louis, says his cocky teammate had the potential to be Hall of Fame material. "Like Bird and Magic, Marvin had all the skills: rebounding, shot blocking, scoring. Not only that, he knew how to use those skills to make his teammates better," says Carr. "He was a special type of player, a maximum-effort guy. And he could talk trash the whole game. But he would always back it up, just like Larry and Magic. He was pretty funny, too."

Away from basketball, however, Barnes began acting entirely differently during his second pro season. "Live hard, die young. That was my motto," he recalls. "I'm being honest. I didn't expect to be around long. I figured I'd probably die in a shootout where I grew up, in the ghetto. I lived for the moment, so I'd drink, use marijuana, and snort cocaine when I could. The coke intensified everything. When I got that rush, I thought the coke was making me a better ballplayer."

Despite his reckless lifestyle, Barnes was a valuable commodity in pro basketball. When the ABA merged with the NBA in 1976, Barnes was taken by Detroit in the first round of the dispersal draft. What the Pistons didn't know, however, was that drugs and alcohol were taking their toll on Barnes.

"I always had been a little bit of a con man. In Detroit, I conned myself," he says, with a forced laugh. "I told everyone I was Superman— and I convinced myself it was true. I got myself to believe I could drink, do drugs, and party all night and still be the old Marvin the next day on the court. I had enough talent to get away with it, because I could still put up good numbers even though I was constantly abusing my body."

His abundance of skill and hustle, coupled with an outgoing personality, kept Barnes a crowd favorite even as his stats declined. Shortly after serving a six-month prison sentence for attempting to carry a gun onto a plane, Barnes asked the Pistons to renegotiate his contract. When the team refused, he demanded to be traded. In November of 1977, Detroit obliged, shipping the discontented starter to Buffalo. After one relatively uneventful season with the Braves, Barnes arrived in Boston.

In his first month with the team, Barnes quickly won over Celtics fans by using his uncanny shot-blocking timing and his above-the-rim rebounding talents to ignite Boston's fastbreak game. Off the court, he charmed the media, which found him to be a proverbial "quote machine."

"People in Boston never forgot how great he was at Providence. When Marvin came to the Celtics, he had everyone rooting for him," said teammate Cedric Maxwell. "He was always smiling and joking with people, from the kids in the stands to the ballboys. You sort of had to like the guy. Plus, he could really play when he wanted to."

But Barnes's desire diminished almost overnight as his appetite for cocaine controlled his life once again. "I was hanging around with all the wrong people. I'd come home from a game and there would be a mountain of coke waiting for me on the dining room table," he recalls. "I didn't even know half the people who came to my home. Didn't matter as long as that coke was there."

The low point of his career came one night at the Garden. "I had just come out of the game and was sitting at the end of the bench," he says. "Before I had come out for warmups, I had stashed a bag of coke into my jacket pocket. Now I put a towel over my head and began snorting the stuff. I think Nate Archibald or Don Chaney saw what I was doing because when I looked up, I saw them both scrambling to sit as far away from me as they could."

Several nights later, following a game in Detroit, Barnes met up with some old acquaintances from his Pistons days, went to an all-night party, and was nowhere to be found when the Celtics boarded their plane for

Boston. When he failed to arrive at the Garden for a game that night, the Celtics decided enough was enough and released him.

Still, Barnes's NBA days weren't over just yet. In the fall of 1979, Clippers coach Gene Shue, a believer in reclamation projects, decided to offer Barnes one last opportunity. The gamble didn't work, as the uninspired, drug-addicted forward averaged only 3.2 points and 3.4 rebounds in 20 games before he was tersely waived.

Alone and broke, Barnes lived on the streets of San Diego. "I figure that conservatively I made about $4 million in the pros. I went through it all. When the Clippers let me go, I was basically homeless. [Clippers teammate] Bill Walton put me up at his place for a while," Barnes says. "But I didn't stay long, because I wanted to go out and score some drugs. That's all I thought about. I was arrested twice for drug possession and once for petty theft. Each time all I got was probation. Finally, I was caught stealing a candy bar and, because of my previous arrests, the judge sent me to jail for three months."

When he was released, Barnes headed east where he briefly returned to his hometown in Providence. Immediately, the city's drug culture reeled him in. "Either I had to get out of there, or the cops were going to get me," he says. "I started drifting, going back to all my old hangouts in Boston, Detroit, and St. Louis. Everywhere I went, I was just looking to get high."

With no income and no savings, Barnes attempted a comeback. "I played half a season with the Detroit Spirits, playing for almost nothing and using drugs the whole time," he admits. "I also played for Trieste in the Italian League. Over there, I got arrested for using [cocaine]. After I was released on bail, I had to sneak across the border to Yugoslavia to avoid going to prison for years."

Returning to the U.S., Barnes eventually decided to check himself into a Houston rehab center that was run by former NBA guard John Lucas, himself a recovering cocaine addict. For a time, it looked like Barnes was conquering his demons.

"I stayed sober for almost two years. I had done so well that I became a counselor at the rehab center," he recalls. "Eventually, though, I did slip, as I used to call it, a number of times. I figure I was in and out of rehab maybe 18 times. Then I noticed that I was constantly feeling weak and tired. I originally figured it was because of the drug use. Finally, I saw a doctor and he told me my liver was damaged, probably from drug and alcohol abuse. That's when I knew I was killing myself. I weighed less than 190 [pounds], just skin and bones. I stopped all the drugs and started eating well. I even got into decent shape by lifting weights. For the first time in years, I was doing all the right things."

Then one day Barnes reluctantly agreed to help a friend obtain some cocaine. The guy kept hounding me. He said, 'Marvin, come on, you know dealers. Just do me this one favor.' After he begged me for days to get him some drugs, I finally caved in, mainly to get him off my back," Barnes explains. With the police watching his every move, he first paid for the drugs and then delivered them. He was immediately arrested for his role in the drug sale. His sentence: seven years in Lynaugh Prison, just outside Fort Stockton, Texas.

"I only served two years and nine months before being paroled—but it was definitely hard time," he says. "The guards, they would let inmates literally fight to the death. It was that brutal. My personal turning point came when I got in a fight with another inmate and started pounding his head into the cement floor. He was bleeding and unconscious when I just stopped because I felt like I was becoming an animal. Believe me, the guards didn't break it up. Right then, on the spot, I said, 'That's enough craziness. No more drugs, no more prison, no more drama in my life.'"

Barnes finished his sentence while at the same time completing his degree requirements in general education from Providence College. Shortly after gaining his release, he moved to Portsmouth, Virginia, and joined the Rev. E.T. Knight's Mount Carmel Baptist Church, where he was baptized.

"Rev. Knight got me on the right spiritual path and made sure I stayed on it," Barnes says. "He made me realize that if I was at peace spiritually, I would have no problem dealing with everything else in life. And he was absolutely right."

Barnes also received financial and personal support from former St. Louis Spirits owner Ozzie Silna. "From the first day I met Ozzie back in 1974, he has always stuck by me—no matter what," he says. "When I was ill, he paid all my medical bills. Each time I would come out of rehab, he'd give me money to help me get a fresh start. And when I got out of prison, he convinced me to talk to the Rev. Knight, which was the best thing I could ever do."

Five years ago, Barnes decided it was time move back to Providence from Virginia. "This time I wasn't worried about having a relapse. I wasn't about to slip again," he says. "I was going home because I had a plan. I wanted to use my experiences to help kids who are growing up in the same type of neighborhoods that I grew up in. I wanted to help them understand why it's important to get an education, stay out of trouble, and keep drugs out of their lives. I knew all the problems they faced. I knew I could reach these kids."

With Silna's support, he founded the Rebound Foundation to counsel inner-city youth. "I mentor 15 boys a year," Barnes says proudly. "I really get on them to do all the right things in school and in their personal lives. I tell them my prison stories, and I let them know that if they think they can handle prison time, they'd better damn well think again. I also bring in judges, ex-prisoners, and ex-gang members to talk to them about the consequences of being a street thug."

The non-profit foundation helps at-risk teens find jobs. It also has a year-round after-school program, which includes basketball practice and games. "And the foundation is going to expand," Barnes, now 54 years old, says proudly and confidently. "We're going to start a similar program for young girls. We're hoping to start programs in other NBA cities."

As he enthusiastically talks of the future, Barnes seems to have found his purpose in life. "I go to church and pray for strength," he says. "I go to AA meetings every week. My goals are simple: No more slips, no more excuses, no more drama. If I reach those goals, I'll be the happiest man on earth."

NATE
ARCHIBALD

Turning Tiny Around

When Nate Archibald was traded to Boston by the San Diego Clippers in the summer of 1978, he wasn't certain he'd make it through even one year in a Celtics uniform. Having missed the entire previous season while recovering from a torn Achilles tendon, the former three-time All-Star justifiably wondered whether, at age 30, he was ancient history. The Celtics, attempting to mount comeback of their own after going 30-52, were willing to gamble that Archibald's fierce competitive nature would eventually drive him to become the "Tiny" of old.

"Fortunately for me, Red [Auerbach] was completely in my corner right from the start," the now 57-year-old Hall of Famer explains. "Before training camp, he just looked me right in the eyes and said, 'Look, there's no sense in pushing yourself too much and risking a setback. I want you back at 100 percent, not 70 or 80 percent. Don't worry about this season, because we're going to stink, with you or without you.' And, boy, was he right. Things were pretty ugly during my first year [in Boston]."

Indisputably, Archibald had once been the NBA's premiere point guard, a clever, intelligent, and mentally tough floor leader. His game was both explosive and fundamentally sound, two descriptions that in today's basketball world are a contradiction in terms. Proof positive of his overall offensive talents came in 1973 when the 6'1" Archibald set a "virtually

AP/WWP

NATE ARCHIBALD

College: Texas-El Paso '70 | Height: 6'1" | Weight: 160 lbs.
Position: Guard | Years with Celtics: 1978-'79 through 1982-'83

Notes: A six-time NBA All-Star and member of the NBA's 50th Anniversary All-Time Team, Archibald is perhaps best known as the only player to lead the NBA in scoring (34.0 ppg) and assists (11.4 apg) in the same season (as a member of Kansas City Kings in 1972-'73). Member of one NBA championship team while with the Boston (1981). Waived on July 22, 1983. Enshrined in the Naismith Memorial Basketball Hall of Fame as a player on May 13, 1991.

untouchable" record by leading the league in both scoring (34.0 points a game) and assists (11.4 per game) in the same season as a member of the Kansas City Kings, not coincidentally coached by another playmaking genius, Bob Cousy, who had selected the UTEP star in second round of the 1970 draft.

"I don't see Tiny's record being broken," says Cousy. "Today's teams don't get enough easy fastbreak baskets. They'd rather run a set offense and have their big star go one-on-one. Unless coaches go back to a faster paced, more wide-open game, Tiny's record is as safe as any. And what makes that record so impressive to me is that Tiny had a pass-first mentality. He certainly wasn't a gunner. The vast majority of his points came off drives to the basket where he'd either get a layup or give up that frail body of his to draw a foul. When he did take a jumper from the outside, it was an open shot. He'd take them and make most of them just to keep his defender off-balance."

The pupil has equally high praise for his first pro coach. "Cousy had faith in me, a lot more than I had in myself as a 21-year-old," recalls Archibald. "He just handed me the ball and said, 'This is your team. Run the show.' A lot of guys get drafted a lot higher than I was and don't play their whole first year. Here I was as a no-name rookie, thinking how lucky I was just to be in the league, starting as the point person. I did what Cooz asked, but I wasn't ready for it. I made more than my share of mistakes, but Cooz would never be anything but positive. It was his coaching which set up my whole career."

But in 1978, as a new member of the Celtics, the lefty guard—all 160 pounds of him—would have to prove to the experts and, more importantly, to himself that he could fit in, still lead a team, and stay healthy. "I had a lot of self-doubt about my speed and quickness," Archibald recalls. "In the back of your mind, you always have thoughts about blowing out the tendon again. The only thing I didn't worry about were the fundamentals. I knew I still had my skills to carry me."

Playing in 69 games, Archibald averaged just 11.0 points and 4.7 assists, both career lows, in his first Celtic season. "I can't say I was satisfied with how I played, but I could live with it. We were one of the worst rebounding teams in the league, so we didn't have much of a fastbreak game," he says with a wry smile. "Our whole offensive game was weak. There was too much individual play and not enough passing. We won just 29 games. …Red was right. We did sort of stink."

Still Archibald was optimistic about his future. "By the end of the season, I was completely healthy. I knew my Achilles problem was in the past," he explains. "For the first time in more than two years, I had no injury issues. I could finally concentrate on just playing. After our final game, Red sat down with me and told me what he wanted me to work on in the offseason. I knew he wanted me back, but he didn't make any promises.

On the day it was announced that former Cavs coach Bill Fitch would take over on the Celtics bench, Archibald received a phone call. "Fitch told me I would be starting," says Archibald, who, as a four-year-old, was nicknamed "Tiny" by his father. "Then he told me to be in 'running shape' because he wanted a fastbreak team. Right then, I knew there were going to be a lot of new faces around."

Including one Larry Joe Bird.

"Because [Bird] was drafted a year before he signed, I had seen him play in college a number of times. I remember there were people who said he can't run, can't jump, and has no quickness," says Archibald. "My reaction was 'Who cares?' The guy did everything right fundamentally. He shot perfectly, passed perfectly, rebounded perfectly. When he showed how good he was as a pro, people started calling him 'Larry Legend.' I always said he was 'Larry The Professor,' because if you watched him, you could learn everything there is to know about how to play the game."

Along with Bird, the Celtics also added second-year center Rick Robey, veteran swingman M.L. Carr, and rookie guard Gerald Henderson. "Even in training camp, which was definitely hell, I knew we had a serious team. It all stemmed from how Bird played the game," Archibald says. "I mean, he'd do something in every game, even in practice, that would make me shake my head and wonder, 'Damn, how did he do that?' When you have a guy who plays with as much confidence as Bird did, everybody just picks up on it."

With Bird earning Rookie of the Year honors, Boston was able to achieve the greatest one-season turnaround in NBA history, going from an embarrassing 29 wins in 1979 to 61 victories in 1980. It was a rebirth not only for the Celtics, but for their point guard, too, who was named to the All-Star team for the first time since 1976. Playing 37 minutes a game and averaging 14.1 points and 8.4 assists, Archibald wore down the opposition with his fastbreak brilliance.

"We had a bunch of guys who loved to rebound and take off," remembers Archibald. "Max [Cedric Maxwell], [Dave] Cowens, Bird, and Robey, they all could go to the boards, make the outlet pass, and beat their man upcourt. That made my job easy because, as the point person, I had a lot of options."

In the Eastern Conference Finals, however, the Celtics were humbled by the Julius Erving-led 76ers, who utilized a well-balanced halfcourt offense to limit Boston's running opportunities and take the series, four games to one. "To get that far and then go totally flat, it was embarrassing," says Archibald. "That whole offseason people asked me the same question I was asking myself: 'What happened?' I didn't have any good answers."

With Boston acquiring Robert Parish and the draft rights to power forward Kevin McHale in The Great Golden State Swindle, Archibald now had two additional offensive weapons at his disposal as the Celtics opened up the 1980-'81 season. "This team had no weaknesses. And because of how we finished up the previous year, we were hungry, even a bit cocky," Archibald explains. "As Maxwell used to tell us when the game was on the line, 'If you're scared, better buy yourself a Doberman.' Well, we weren't scared of any team."

The Celtics and rival Philly both won 62 games in the regular season. Then the two teams again faced each other in the conference finals. Down three games to one, the Celtics staged what is considered the NBA's most exciting and greatest comeback, winning the final three games of the series by a total of five points.

"I still remember Red coming into the locker room in Philadelphia after we had lost Game 4. We were all upset, but he was very calm," recalls

Archibald. "He looked at us for a second and then told us, 'Look, this series isn't over. They still have to win one more game to beat you. One more game. Don't let them win that one more game. It's that simple.' And that's how we approached the rest of the series."

The title matchup against Houston was truly anticlimactic, with the Celtics winning championship No. 14 in a six-game series as Tiny's penetration moves produced 13 points and 12 assists in the clinching game.

"Without a doubt, the greatest moment in my career," says Archibald. "To be a part of that team with all the great players we had is something I am very proud of. The year I led the league in points and assists doesn't compare to being on a championship team, because I didn't help the Kings win a thing. We didn't even make the playoffs the year I set that record. That's why individual stats have never impressed me too much."

Compiling a 63-19 regular-season record the following year, the Celtics seemed to be on track for a title repeat. However, in Game 3 of the Conference Finals against the 76ers, Archibald suffered what would be a series-ending left shoulder injury. Without its backcourt leader, Boston fell to Philly in seven games.

"Very depressing," Archibald recalls. "I couldn't raise my shooting arm. I even practiced shooting righty, but I knew I couldn't help the team."

Archibald's Celtic career came to an abrupt and unpleasant end following Milwaukee's four-game sweep of Boston in the 1983 Eastern Conference semifinals. Fitch had decided to use the 34-year-old playmaker as a sixth man rather than a starter in the Bucks series. Although the coach stressed that the move would enable Archibald to be fresher and more productive in crucial moments of the game, especially during crunch time, the veteran guard was quietly steaming. "I wouldn't mind if someone beat me out for my starter's role. But to just have it taken away...that's not right," he said moments before the series began.

Two months after the Celtics' collapse against the Bucks, the six-time All-Star was unceremoniously waived. He finished his career by playing 51 games with Milwaukee the following season before quietly retiring. "It wasn't the way I hoped to go out," he says, "but I had a great career doing what I loved."

Not surprisingly, a primary focus of Archibald's life after pro basketball is helping inner-city youth understand the importance of gaining an education. As a player, Archibald would spend his offseasons coaching youth basketball in the South Bronx, where he had grown up.

"It's not a pretty neighborhood. Many of the buildings are completely burnt out. There's poverty, crime, and drugs everywhere," he says. "It's hard for kids here to realize that the world can open up to them. That's one of the things I emphasize, that they can improve themselves through basketball and an education."

Said South Bronx community worker Hilton Barker, "Once [basketball players] make it, they're gone. Once they get the big car, they point it out of here. Except for Tiny. He came back."

But not just to teach basketball. Even today, it is not unusual for Archibald to spend his summer nights buying pizza and soda for kids and just talking to them for hours about subjects ranging from music to school to drug use.

"Because I was a pro athlete, kids listen to me," he explains. "My big advantage is that I'm in the community every chance I get. No one drools over me. Because of what I've done with my life, they listen to me. When they need help, they know they can come to me without being shy, because I'm just a guy who hangs around with them. We're on the same level. It's just friend-to-friend relationships.

"I don't preach to the kids, I just talk with them. I tell them about opportunities for scholarships, student loans, and grants—even if they don't play basketball. I'm realistic, though. I know I can't help everybody. You might have a group of 15 kids, and only two or three will make it to some degree of success. It's just a sad fact that some of them are not going to be able to leave [the South Bronx]."

Given his dedication to helping youngsters both on and off the basketball court, it is not surprising that Archibald, after spending five years as an assistant coach at Georgia, decided to pursue a career in education. After obtaining his master's degree, Archibald became a teacher at P.S. 175 in the Bronx. In his spare time, he worked at the Harlem Men's Shelter.

A member of the NBA's 50th Anniversary All-Time Team, Archibald has coached in the ABA, NBDL, and, most recently, the USBL with the Brevard Blue Ducks. He has yet to get an opportunity to coach at the NBA level. "I'd certainly listen to any offers," he says, "but there just haven't been any yet."

The problem, according to Cousy, is that NBA coaches still belong to a "Good Old Boys" fraternity. "Tiny just isn't a self-promoter or a guy who 'networks.' He's not the type of person who walks into a room with a big smile and starts shaking hands with everybody. He's still shy, maybe somewhat insecure. What's obvious is that he has a great knowledge of the game and he can communicate that knowledge, especially to younger players. He'd make a hell of a coach if someone gives him the chance."

While he waits for an opportunity, Archibald, who worked in the NBA's community relations department the past two years, continues to coach youth basketball in both Harlem and the South Bronx.

"I'm not a big fan of AAU programs," he says. "Coaches go all out to recruit the best talent. Then they just go and throw a ball onto the court and say, 'Okay, start playing.' Their teams win, but the kids themselves lose because they aren't learning a thing about the fundamentals of the game. That's not what youth basketball should be about."

Currently residing in the New York City area, Archibald continues to lead by example. Now 57 years old, he is close to completing his requirements for a doctorate in education. Dr. Tiny will no doubt continue to work on a cure for what ails today's inner-city youth.